Thomas Cook

Publishing

BUDAPEST

BY
LOUIS JAMES

Produced by
Thomas Cook Publishing

Written by Louis James
Original photography by Ken Patterson

Edited and designed by Laburnum Technologies Pvt Ltd
C-533 Triveni Apts, Sheikh Sarai Phase 1, New Delhi 110

Published by Thomas Cook Publishing
A division of Thomas Cook Holdings Ltd

PO Box 227, The Thomas Cook Business Park,
Units 19–21, Coningsby Road,
Peterborough PE3 8XX, United Kingdom
E-mail: books@thomascook.com
www.thomascookpublishing.com

ISBN: 1-841572-65-9

Head of Publishing: Donald Greig
Project Editor: Charlotte Christensen
Project Administrator: Michelle Warrington
DTP: Steven Collins

Series Consultant: Vivien Stone
Series Manager: Stephen York

Printed and bound in Spain by: Grafo Industrias Gráficas, Basauri.

Cover: Parliament building and Danube River.
Photograph by Gavin Hellier/Robert Harding Picture Library.
Inside cover: photographs supplied by Spectrum Colour Library.

CD manufacturing services provided by business interactive ltd,
Rutland, UK.

Contents

Introduction

At the end of the 19th century a traveller to Budapest neatly described the enigmatic quality of the city: 'If one is travelling from the east in the direction of Western Europe, it is in Budapest that one experiences the breath of Western civilisation. However, if one is travelling in the opposite direction, it is here that one first gets a taste of the East . . .' When the seven Magyar (Hungarian) tribes came over the Carpathians more than 1,000 years ago, one group of them pitched their tents at this strategic point on the mighty River Danube. Although they were always to retain a proud memory of their Asian origins, they now began a new and settled existence in Europe.

In the Middle Ages the Royal Castle of Buda and its ancillary town grew wealthy under Magyar, Anjou (Angevin), and Luxembourg rulers. The subsequent 150-year long Turkish occupation, and the Habsburg rule that followed, then reduced

On the banks of the River Danube

WHAT IT MEANS TO BE A MAGYAR

'Anyone who wants to understand Hungary,' writes the poet and journalist István Eörsi, 'needs to find the answer to one great secret: how is it that this country has survived at all? . . . No nation is so experienced in defeat as the Hungarians.' This feeling of being the victims of history is recurrent in the Magyar psyche.

On two occasions in the past – when the Tartars invaded in the 13th century and during the Turkish occupation – there was a real danger of national extinction. In the 18th century the German philosopher, Johann Herder, predicted that the Magyar nation and culture would soon disappear, absorbed by their Slav and German neighbours.

It is language that most isolates Hungarians. Arthur Koestler summed up the fears and contradictions in the Magyars' image of themselves: 'To be Hungarian is a collective neurosis.'

done to make the city hum again. With three elections behind them and the highest rate of foreign investment in the former Eastern Bloc, the people of Hungary have crossed the Millennium with grounds for optimism, despite the shadow of poverty.

However, don't expect Hungarians to admit that things have improved. As the local saying goes: 'A pessimist is only a well-informed optimist'.

Buda to provincial status. In the mid-19th century the hitherto insignificant town of Pest rapidly expanded into a great industrial metropolis. Until around 1860, half its inhabitants were German-speaking and there was also a large influx of Jews; most of the latter rapidly assimilated and became leading figures in the arts and in business. By 1900, Buda and Pest (united since 1873) had acquired the patina of mixed culture and unbridled capitalism which has now reappeared after 40 years of suspended animation under Communism.

Back to the Future

As in other cities of the former Eastern Bloc, the gap between the haves and have-nots has widened rapidly since 1989.

New luxury hotels have been built and Western car models stand gleaming in showrooms; but there are also the homeless, the beggars, and the hard-pressed pensioners.

On the credit side, Hungarians are natural entrepreneurs and much is being

A Károly Lotz mosaic on Clark Ádám tér depicting the coat of arms of the Kindgom of Hungary

The Land

Budapest lies 47 degrees 23 minutes north and 19 degrees 9 minutes east, on either side of the River Danube (Duna). Within the river's 28-km passage through the city, the width of the channel varies between 1km and 230m. The mighty waterway has shaped the character of the city. For the Romans it was a defensive barrier – they built their garrison and administrative capital at Aquincum on the western bank. The Magyar kings shifted the focus to the natural citadel of Buda Hill, while Pest was the gateway to the east, a town of travellers and traders, later the dynamic centre of business and industry.

THOMAS COOK'S BUDAPEST

In 1885, Cook's were appointed official travel agents for the agricultural exhibition staged by the Hungarian government. The first Thomas Cook office in Budapest was opened three years later. Cook's were active in promoting Hungary's Millennial exhibition in 1896, and Budapest spas in the 1930s.

In the landscape, too, the characteristics of the two cities reflect different aspects of Hungary: from the flattish terrain of Pest, the Alföld (Great Hungarian Plain) stretches to the east and south; on the west bank the gentle hills of Buda (the highest is the 529m János-hegy) point the way to the rolling landscapes of Transdanubia.

Economy

Hungary has nearly completed a painful restructuring of its economy following the collapse of Communism and the disappearance of traditional markets in the Eastern Bloc. Inflation is too high at around 7–8 per cent and there is still a current account deficit of around $2 billion. But economic recovery is now palpable, with a growth rate of 4.7 per cent, achieved by restructuring and substantial reorientation of exports away from Russia, although Hungary was still hit by the 1998 economic crisis in Russia. The service sector has been revitalised thanks to substantial foreign investment. Money from abroad is also helping other industries, such as breweries and automobile factories.

Environment

Like other former Eastern Bloc cities, Budapest suffers from a decaying infrastructure and serious pollution. In 1992 academics and lawyers formed an Environmental Management and Law Association in an attempt to push environmental concerns to the top of the political agenda.

Another initiative, by the mayor of Budapest, offered owners of smoke-belching two-stroke Trabants free passes for public transport and low-interest loans if they gave up their cars. A start has also been made on cleaning up energy production: the Kelenföld power station, which supplies 36,000 homes, has been rebuilt for gas turbine production of electricity, using waste gases to heat the boilers at a cost of $100 million. The reduction in sulphur dioxide was about 80 per cent, in nitrogen oxide 40 per cent.

Budapest's water supply was endangered by the Slovak government's decision to persist with the Gabcikovo hydroelectric dam on the Danube, a legacy of totalitarian planning. Hungary pulled out of the project in 1992, refusing to complete the complementary dam at Nagymaros on Hungarian territory. The fertile agricultural area of Szigetköz in western Hungary is already badly affected. However, the reduction of fuel emissions and the cleaning of public buildings have given Budapest a new face.

Investment in infrastructure will take longer, but the telephone system has been modernised (every second Magyar now has a mobile phone). Among the new roads being built to stop lorries thundering through built-up areas is the M0 motorway which, when complete, will form a ring around Budapest.

Goodbye Trabi!

An elegiac piece in the press of 1991 lamented the passing of East German imports – the 'Trabi' (Trabant), which provided an experience 'like riding a four-wheel moped in a raincoat'; the Practica 35mm SLR, 'a good workhorse camera designed for planets without gravity'; and 'nifty kitchen wares made of slag-iron'.

Pollution has taken a heavy toll of many of Pest's façades

History

AD 106	The Roman garrison of Aquincum (in Óbuda) becomes the capital of Lower Pannonia.
5th century	According to legend, Attila the Hun ruled from the abandoned Roman amphitheatre in Aquincum. His brother, Bleda, is supposed to have given his name to a new city – 'Buda'.
896	Seven Magyar tribes under Árpád cross the Carpathians and settle on the Danubian plains.
Late 10th century	The Magyar Prince Géza converts to Christianity; his son Vajk is baptised as István (Stephen).
1000	Stephen is crowned King of Hungary on Christmas Day, with a crown sent by the Pope. Between 997 and 1038, King (later Saint) Stephen turns Hungary into a Christian feudal state.
1061	The first documentary reference about Pest.
1241	Tartar (Mongol) invaders virtually destroy Hungary. To rebuild it, King Béla IV invites Germans and other foreigners to settle. The Castle of Buda is built (1247–65).
1301	The Hungarian Árpád line dies out. The House of Anjou succeeds, followed by Sigismund of Luxembourg in 1387.
1458–90	Under Matthias I (Corvinus), Buda achieves its golden age.
1526–41	Buda falls to the Turks.
1686	Armies led by Charles of Lorraine and Eugene of Savoy reconquer Buda. Hungary falls under Habsburg rule.
1710–11	Buda and Pest are blockaded during the War of Independence waged by Ferenc Rákóczi II.
1795	A Jacobin revolt is crushed. Archduke Joseph (son of Leopold II) becomes Palatine (Viceroy) of Hungary.
1848	Hungary, under Lajos Kossuth, briefly achieves independence from Habsburg rule.
1867	Franz Joseph and Ferenc Deák negotiate the

Ausgleich (Compromise) to create the Austro-Hungarian Empire.

1872–3	The towns of Buda, Óbuda, and Pest are united to form Budapest.
1896	The Millennial Celebrations mark 1,000 years of Hungary's existence.
1918–19	The Austro-Hungarian Empire collapses; the Hungarian Republic is proclaimed. The Communist Republic of Councils is formed, before Admiral Miklós Horthy becomes Regent.
1920	By the Treaty of Trianon, Hungary loses two-thirds of its territory. Three million Hungarians are marooned in the Empire's successor states.
1945–48	Soviet armies 'liberate' Budapest; the Communists seize power.
1956	Soviet Army invades Hungary to suppress a popular anti-Commuist rebellion. János Kádár forms a puppet regime.
1988	Kádár is ousted, an interim government of

reform Communists works for free elections.

1990	Right-of-centre Hungarian Democratic Forum led by József Antall wins elections.
1990–94	Sweeping market reforms, but living standards fall.
1994	Socialists and Free Democrats win elections.
1998	The right-of-centre Hungarian Civic Party under Viktor Orbán forms a government with the Smallholders' Party.
2002	Socialists and Free Democrats win elections again.

Statue of St Stephen on Castle Hill

1 9 5 6 a n d A l l T h a t

The heroism of the Hungarian revolution of 1956 has passed into history – a brave battle against appalling odds. For a few brief days of euphoria, it looked as if it might succeed, and the Stalinist tyranny seemed on the brink of extinction.

Pressure for change came first from the so-called 'Petőfi Circle', named after Hungary's national poet and freedom fighter. Then student demonstrations attracted thousands of supporters. Finally, factory workers became the driving force of the revolution. Much of the Hungarian army, led by Pál Maléter, also fought for freedom.

TIMETABLE OF A REVOLUTION
6 October 1956

200,000 people attend the reburial of László Rajk, the Interior Minister executed after a show-trial by the Rákosi regime.

23 October

In solidarity with the Polish opposition, students lead a march to the statue of the Polish general and Hungarian freedom fighter, József Bem.

At 6pm, Imre Nagy, previously expelled from the Party for his espousal of a more humane government as prime minister in 1953,

speaks to vast crowds before the Parliament.

At 11pm, students besiege the radio station and the ÁVH (Security Service) open fire on them.

24 October

Imre Nagy becomes prime minister. Soviet tanks move on to Budapest.

31 October

A truce is arranged and Soviet tanks withdraw.

1 November

Nagy announces that Hungary is to leave the Warsaw Pact.

3 November

Pál Maléter, negotiating with the Soviet Army under guarantee of safe conduct, is arrested.

4 November

Soviet Army reinvades. János Kádár announces the formation of his puppet government. Nagy flees to the Yugoslav embassy.

22 November

Nagy leaves the Yugoslav embassy with a promise of safe conduct and is arrested.

16 June 1958

Nagy and Maléter are executed.

AFTERMATH OF THE REVOLUTION

While the borders remained open, 200,000 people fled the country. There were an estimated 2,000 revenge executions; thousands more were imprisoned.

16 June 1989

Some 250,000 people attended a ceremony on Heroes' Square to honour Imre Nagy and Pál Maléter, whose remains were reburied.

6 July 1989

On the day the Supreme Court declared Nagy innocent of the charges on which he was convicted and executed, János Kádár died.

'If my life is necessary to prove that not all Communists are enemies of the people, then I willingly give it up.' IMRE NAGY, reportedly his last words in 1958.

Governance

In 1989 the satellite regimes of Soviet Russia buckled one by one under the combined pressure of failing economies and Mikhail Gorbachev's policy of *glasnost* (openness). The smooth transition from totalitarianism to democracy was possible in Hungary, chiefly because the last Communist government accepted the inevitable gracefully.

Interior of Parliament

The End of Communism

During János Kádár's long rule (1956–88), the oppressive paraphernalia of Stalinism had been softened and a small private sector allowed to develop. This had led to Hungary being regarded as 'the happiest barracks in the Socialist camp'. But in the 1980s, the country suffered from rising inflation and an alarming increase in foreign debt. The ageing Kádár compounded his economic mismanagement by the decision to go ahead with the construction of an ecologically catastrophic dam at Nagymaros on the Danube, part of a joint energy project with the Slovaks.

At the May 1988 Party Congress, reformers and technocrats joined forces to oust Kádár from the leadership. By July 1989 four of them, under the impressive leadership of the youthful Miklós Németh, were in control of the government. By October the Communists had reconstituted themselves as the Socialist Party, the 'iron curtain' on the Austrian border had been dismantled, and free elections announced for the following year. In November, on the 33rd anniversary of

the 1956 revolution (*see pp10–11*), the Republic of Hungary was proclaimed.

The Elections of 1990

Two parties dominated the second round of voting (25 March): the populist and conservative Hungarian Democratic Forum and the intellectual metropolitan Alliance of Free Democrats, with the Democratic Forum emerging a clear winner. A worrying sign was the low turn-out, which seemed to indicate that much of the electorate expected very little to be achieved by any political grouping. The government subsequently formed by József Antall was a coalition that included the revived Smallholders' Party (winners of the last free elections in 1945, but now a sentimental relic) and the Christian Democrats. A distinguished Free Democrat and former Communist victim, Árpád Göncz, was elected president by Parliament.

The Antall Government

In facing the severe economic and political problems inherited from Communism, the Antall government looked increasingly beleaguered. Its image was also tarnished by the right wing of the Democratic Forum, led by the writer István Csurka, indulging in anti-Semitic rhetoric and demanding witch-hunts against former Communists.

Until his death in December 1993, Antall ploughed on with his strategy of gradual adjustment to the free market economy. But while fiscal retrenchment and conscientious debt servicing have preserved Hungary's credit rating on the financial markets, inflation at over 20 per cent, high unemployment, and social hardship produced a Socialist victory in the 1994 elections.

Hungary at the Crossroads

As Hungary enters the 21st century, there are many negative factors in Hungarian life. The economy has been buffeted by the world recession and the reluctance of the European Union to admit competitively priced Hungarian products. Society has been hamstrung by the contrast between the poverty of many and the wealth of a few. The public frequently turns in disgust from politicians seemingly more interested in the spoils of power than in the enlightened use of it. Yet there are also grounds for optimism. Hungarians are entrepreneurial and resourceful as a nation: if the opportunities arise, they will be quick to seize them.

Growth has recommenced and the country has attracted the most foreign investment of the former Eastern Bloc countries. A youthful and pragmatic government was appointed in 1998, although hampered by an arch-conservative coalition partner. Fresh elections in 2002 returned the Socialists and Free Democrats to power, with Péter Medgyesi made Prime Minister.

Freedom
Monument on
Gellért-hegy

People and Culture

The numerous warm, healing springs of the Budapest area attracted settlers from earliest times, the first of them occupying the limestone caves formed by spa waters on the Danube's west bank. Eventually these spas (*see pp38–9*) were to become a significant source of wealth for the inhabitants. The Danube itself was crucial to the development of Hungary, bringing trade and valuable immigrants, as well as less welcome invaders and floods.

A game of chess adds variety to a visit to the spa

The historic name of the Hungarian people is 'Magyars', 'Hungary' being 'Magyarország'. Now much diluted, the Magyars are descended from the Ugrian branch of the Finno-Ugric people who once populated the land between the Urals and the River Ob. While their northern cousins, the Finns and Estonians, are descendants of the group that migrated north and west around 2000 BC, the Magyars were influenced by Turkic and other cultures around the Caucasus before crossing into the Carpathian Basin in AD 896.

City Population

Buda and Pest have had a mixed population since early times, including foreign craftsmen and merchants. Large numbers of Germans were settled by the Austrian Empress Maria Theresa in order to rebuild the country after 150 years of Turkish devastation: then in the 19th century thousands of Jews migrated to Hungary from Moravia and Galicia, the majority settling in Pest.

Today, the population of Budapest is nearly two million, one in five of the Hungarians living within Hungary. Some five million live beyond the borders, most of them as minorities in neighbouring countries. Movement out of Budapest to the wider conurbation is increasing.

Religion

Hungary has been Christian since the 11th century, when King Stephen forcibly converted the population. Although Orthodoxy had a toehold of influence through royal marriages, the country was firmly Catholic until the Reformation, but 90 per cent of Hungarians had become Protestant by the late 16th century. Habsburg rule and its attendant Counter-Reformation sought to reverse this situation, but Protestantism hung on in the east and on the Great Plain. Today, Hungary is 57 per cent Catholic and 30 per cent Protestant.

A European Culture

Hungary's artistic legacy reflects the country's attachment to the traditions of Western European culture, and the further back we look, the more apparent

Statue of Franz Liszt by László Martou on the square named after him

this becomes. From the establishment of the feudal state under King Stephen (997–1038) until the Turkish invasions in the 16th century, Hungary was part of the supra-national European Christian culture. Artists and craftsmen came from the Low Countries, Germany, and Italy to work for the Hungarian kings of the late Árpád, Anjou, and Luxembourg dynasties. The Cistercian, Benedictine, and Premonstratensian orders built churches in the pan-European Romanesque and Gothic styles: fine examples have survived at Ják in Western Hungary and Bélapátfalva in the east.

The palaces of Buda and Visegrád (*see p48 & p125*) reached the summit of splendour under King Matthias Corvinus (1458–90), who invited the best Italian craftsmen to work there. His Renaissance court was a glittering centre of the arts and humanist scholarship. Half a century later Hungary was dismembered in the Turkish wars; Transylvania retained its political and cultural autonomy under the leadership of Protestant princes, but the rest of the territory was carved up between the Turks and the Habsburgs.

The Rise of National Culture

The expulsion of the Turks at the end of the 17th century brought with it the Counter-Reformation and Habsburg dominance.

The Baroque town of Buda and Baroque churches in Pest date from this period. National resistance to the Austrian oppressors was conducted through warfare in the 18th century, but increasingly found expression through culture after Emperor Joseph II (1780–90) tried to Germanise his Hungarian subjects. The epics of Mihály Vörösmarty (1800–55) revived consciousness of Magyar history and the poet Sándor Petőfi became a hero of the 1848 war of independence against the Habsburgs. The early 19th-century architecture of Pest, while reflecting the Central European taste for Neo-Classicism, was created by Hungarian masters such as Mihály Pollack and József Hild. Later in the 19th century, Miklós Ybl built many of the great Neo-Renaissance palaces on the graceful boulevards of the expanding city.

Back to the Roots

In the late-19th century, we encounter a different kind of Hungarian self-perception, one that reconciles semi-mythical Eastern roots with Western civilisation. The national revival in literature began with the proclamation by Ferenc Kölcsey (author of the Hungarian national anthem) that poetry must be sought 'in the songs of the common people', while in the late 19th century architects and artists began to

Statue of Béla Bartók in the garden of his house

A beautiful view of Budapest from János-hegy (St John's Hill) in the Buda Hills

cultivate a consciously Hungarian manner. Ödön Lechner (*see pp68–9*) was one such architect, and Károly Kós (*see p139*), in the early years of the 20th century, drew inspiration from Transylvanian vernacular forms and the English Arts and Crafts movement. The latter also influenced the members of the Gödöllő artists' colony, founded in 1902 near Budapest, whose work exploited Hungarian folk motifs. In the fine arts the *plein air* school of Nagybánya produced distinctively Hungarian landscape paintings, while the idiosyncratic work of Tivadar Csontváry Kosztka embodied a mystical sense of Hungarian identity.

In music, Franz Liszt was the first to popularise Hungarian themes. He also founded the Budapest Music Academy, which was to nurture innumerable great talents. In 1905 Béla Bartók and Zoltán Kodály began their great work of systematically collecting Hungarian folk music from all over the country and this was to influence their own music.

Impressions

The outskirts of Budapest are little different from those of other cities of the former Eastern Bloc: decaying factories ring the Pest side and blocks of prefabricated 'panel housing' disfigure the skyline. Luckily, Budapest is still a modest-sized city by contemporary European standards and the centre is quickly reached from the airport.

A cheap ride to and from the airport

The historic cores of Pest and Buda hug opposite banks of the Danube. You can gain an overall impression of them by taking one of the trams that run along either side of the river (from Jászai Mari tér or Batthyány tér); or you could climb to the Halászbástya (Fishermen's Bastion) on Castle Hill for a bird's-eye view of Pest.

Pest is a bustling, lively town with towering 19th-century blocks and great boulevards. At first it is easy to get lost in the urban density of the Belváros (Inner City); but a few minutes' walk in any direction brings you to a major landmark, square, or avenue. By contrast, residential Buda is on a smaller scale and more private, while Castle Hill is an historical tableau.

In his *Budapest Walks* in 1916, city chronicler Gyula Krúdy wrote: 'This city smells of violets in the spring, as do the ladies along the promenade above the river on the Pest side. In the fall, it is Buda that suggests the tone: the odd thud of chestnuts dropping on the castle walk, fragments of the music of a military band wafting over the forlorn silence: autumn and Buda were born of the same mother.' Today, though a Transylvanian fiddler may have replaced

the military band and ladies on the promenade are redolent of high fashion names like Gucci or Benetton rather than the scent of violets, nostalgia is in: Budapest is selling old style to a new clientele.

When to Go

Central Europe's continental climate is extremely hot in summer, raw and cold in winter. The nicest times to visit are between April and the end of June and, especially, between September and the end of October. The long Indian summer provides ideal weather for excursions (*see p122*). If you must visit in high summer, you can keep cool by heading for the spas (*see pp38–9*) during the heat of the day and lodging in the Buda Hills rather than down in the stifling city. August sees the spectacular fireworks display above the Danube which usually marks the beginning of the end of the *canicula* – as Hungarians call the broiling mid-summer season.

The Budapest Arts Weeks kick off on the anniversary of Béla Bartók's birth (25 September). Annual events include a wine festival, an international dog show in May, and the Budapest Spring Festival in the second half of March.

Arriving

Direct flights from European capitals and America arrive at Ferihegy, Budapest's international airport, 16km to the east of the city centre. Budapest has several daily rail connections to Vienna, trains arriving and leaving from the Déli pályaudvar (Southern Railway Station) or the Keleti pályaudvar (Eastern Railway Station) according to the time of day. Both have direct metro connections to the centre, as does the Nyugati pályaudvar (Western Railway Station), which serves Prague. From April to October a hydrofoil runs once or twice daily on the Danube between Vienna and Budapest, taking five and a half hours.

The majority of travellers by car arrive via Vienna, which is well served by the German/Austrian Autobahn network. A new motorway now runs from Vienna to Budapest, the Hungarian section being a toll road. An Autobahn sticker must be purchased for the Austrian section (available at petrol stations and special sales points after crossing the border). Make sure that your registration number is carefully recorded on it.

The Western Railway Station

Getting Around

Getting around in Budapest is no great problem for the visitor, although unpronounceable names may cause difficulties at first. The areas of interest to visitors are relatively small and compact, and are well served by metro, trams, trolley buses, and buses. It is advisable to buy an up-to-date street plan on arrival – as late as 1993 some street names were still being changed, although in some cases the old name (with a red line through it) has been left beside the new. It is worth buying the modestly priced three-day excursion ticket (*Háromnapos túristajegy*), valid on all forms of city transport and on sale at larger metro stations. The Budapest Card, valid for 48 or 72 hours, includes not only public transport, but also free admission to 60 museums and other sights, as well as eligibility for discounts at various places.

The metro has three lines, colour coded blue, red, and yellow, and all meet at the central junction on Deák Ferenc tér. The blue line runs across Pest, the red one crosses the Danube to south Buda, and the yellow follows the radial Andrássy út through the centre of Pest.

Trabants can still be seen on the streets

Chain Bridge (Széchenyi lánchíd)

Trolley buses run only on the Pest side. Trams run along either side of the Danube, along the Pest boulevards and on main arteries elsewhere. There is also an excellent bus service, but be aware that you need to press the button near the door if you wish to get off, and also the button outside the door, in newer buses, if the door has not opened and you wish to board the bus. The HÉV suburban railway is useful for excursions (to Szentendre from Batthyány tér or Ráckeve from Kőzvágóhíd, *see p130 & p136*). More transport details are given in the **Practical Guide** on page 188.

Other means of transport in Budapest are principally for sightseeing. The boats criss-crossing the Danube afford views of the Országház (Parliament) and Buda Castle from the river; a cable car (Sikló) runs up to Castle Hill from Clark Ádám tér; a chairlift takes you from Zugliget to János-hegy in the Buda Hills; a cogwheel railway (Fogaskerekű) runs from Városmajor on the Buda side up to

Széchenyi-hegy (Széchenyi Hill); the Children's Railway (*see p154*) runs through the Buda woods.

Taxis are cheap by western standards. There are rather too many rogues – stick to the well-established companies: Budataxi, City Taxi, and Főtaxi (which has the best reputation).

Manners and Mores

Hungarians do not expect foreigners to master their language, but it is best to learn greetings, which are always offered on entering or leaving a shop or in addressing strangers. These are: *jó reggelt kívánok* (good morning), *jó napot kívánok* (good day – from about 10am), *jó estét kívánok* (good evening), and *jó éjszakát kívánok* (goodnight). *Viszontlátásra* is goodbye (*see* Language in the **Practical Guide**). Silence or a nod could be taken as rudeness.

When you introduce yourself or are introduced always shake hands and say your complete name. Your interlocutor will do likewise, but remember that Hungarian names are in reverse order, whether written or spoken. Thus, Englishman John Smith meets Hungarian Kovács János (Smith John).

Hungarians are extremely hospitable and proud housewives will probably press on you more food than you want. Trying to foot the bill in a restaurant is usually a struggle – accept *force majeure* with good grace unless there are compelling reasons for not doing so. If you are invited to somebody's home, flowers for the hostess and perhaps wine for the host are usual. You may be asked to remove your shoes and put on house slippers – simply to protect the invariably spotless home! When it comes to the meal, never drink before your host has raised his glass and wished everyone good health.

Feminists will note that male chauvinism is alive and well, often masquerading as old-style gallantry. Yet battle-hardened ladies have been known to melt just a little when greeted with '*kezét csókolom*' (I kiss your hand).

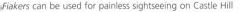

Fiakers can be used for painless sightseeing on Castle Hill

Budapest

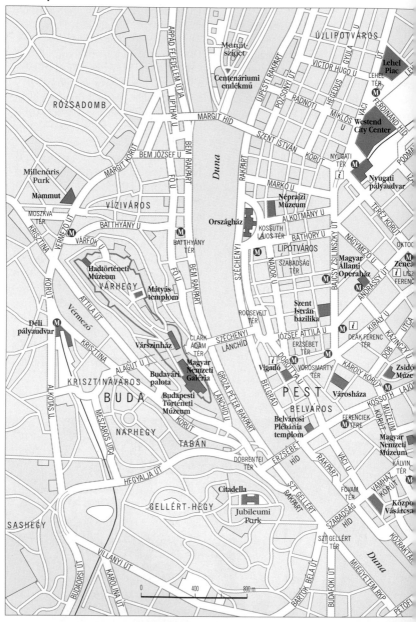

AREAS OF BUDAPEST
Administration

For administrative purposes Budapest is divided into 23 districts, of which about 10 will be of interest to the visitor. The others are primarily residential or industrial. District numbers are required for post codes, but otherwise people stick to names sanctioned by custom and use.

Districts of Buda

The Buda side of the Danube is dominated by Várhegy (Castle Hill), below which is Víziváros (Water Town) stretching as far as Moszkva tér behind the hill's northern tip.

To the northwest is Rózsadomb (the Hill of Roses), where the most sought-after villas are to be found. Further north is Óbuda, and to the south, beyond Gellért-hegy (Gellért Hill), is the rather bleak suburb of Kelenföld; beyond that is an area half developed for the World Exhibition (planned in the 1990s) which was later abandoned.

Districts of Pest

Central Pest is divided by two boulevards, unofficially known as Kiskörút (Little Ringroad, running laterally from Margit híd to Szabadság híd) and Nagykörút (Greater Ringroad, running in a wider arc from Margit híd to Petőfi híd). The fifth district is enclosed by the Little Ringroad and contains the major sights, although some lie between the two boulevards. Further east are the City Woodland Park (Városliget), the sports stadia of Istvánmező, and the Kerepesi temető (Kerepesi Cemetery see pp60–61).

BUDA

Gellért Hill and the small plateau of the Buda Castle with its adjacent town rise on the west bank of the Danube. Between the plateau and the river is a narrow strip of land settled since the Middle Ages and known as Víziváros (Water Town). To the north is Óbuda (Old Buda, *see p28*).

Gellért-hegy (Gellért Hill)

This dolomite rock (235m high) was the earliest inhabited part of Budapest. In prehistoric times, cave-dwellers took advantage of the hot springs bursting through a geological fault – springs that still supply the Gellért spa today. In Roman times, the surviving Celts lived in this area, some 2km from the military and civil settlements of Aquincum to the north. Nowadays the hill is an agreeable park (*see p58*) with footpaths winding up to the Freedom Monument and Citadella on the summit. The grotto chapel (just above the Gellért Hotel) has recently been reconsecrated, after being walled up by the Communists (who, incidentally, located their command bunker, for use in the event of Armageddon, in the bowels of the Gellért rock).

Várhegy (Castle Hill)

The town and fortress of Buda only achieved real significance in the second half of the 10th century. Of the four ancient royal and religious centres in Hungary – Székesfehérvár, Esztergom (*see p124*), Veszprém and Buda – the last to develop was Buda. An economic boom in the 11th and 12th centuries led to expansion of Buda, Óbuda, and Pest,

The church of Krisztínaváros from Castle Hill

and an increase in religious foundations. The Tartar invasion of 1241 devastated the whole region, but thereafter, King Béla IV, known as the refounder of the nation, encouraged settlers from abroad and built the first fortress on Buda Hill.

The Rise of Buda

The basic layout of the town of Buda, which has endured until today, dates from the last third of the 13th century, when the two-storeyed Gothic houses for wealthy burghers were built. Buda had two communities: the Germans, whose Church of Our Lady (later the Matthias Church) stood to the south; and the Hungarians, whose Church of Mary Magdalene was at the northern end.

The first Anjou king, Charles Robert (1308–42), chose to build his great palace upstream of Buda at Visegrád (*see p125*), and it was not until 1347 that Louis I ('the Great') moved his court to Buda and major expansion of the Royal

Palace began. Sigismund of Luxembourg (1387–1437) built a lavish new palace in the 15th century and invited masters from Paris, Stuttgart, and Augsburg to decorate it. The apotheosis was reached under Matthias Corvinus (1458–90), whose Italian masons and craftsmen created the most glittering royal court in contemporary Europe.

Decline and Restoration

After the Turkish conquest of 1541, churches were vandalised and turned into mosques; Buda slowly decayed until its liberation by Habsburg troops in 1686, though the reconquest itself left most of the town in ruins. Subsequently, a small Baroque Buda grew up, together with a very plain and functional Baroque palace, erected under Maria Theresa.

In the late 18th and early 19th centuries, high-ranking officials lived in Buda and the Diet (parliament) met there (for the last time in 1807). While Pest expanded rapidly, Buda stagnated, although areas bordering on Castle Hill, such as Krisztinaváros and Rózsadomb, became desirable residential areas. The last rebuilding of the Royal Palace took place after the 1867 Ausgleich (Compromise) with the Habsburgs that created the Austro-Hungarian Empire. Subsequently, Buda was destroyed by the Russian siege at the end of World War II and rebuilt in the 1950s and 1960s as a showcase of historic restoration.

Strolling on the bastions of Castle Hill

PEST

The origins of Pest lie in the Roman period, when a small fortress to protect the ferry crossing at the narrows was built at what is now the Pest end of the Erzsébet híd (Elizabeth Bridge). In the late 10th century traders settled near the ferry to exploit the Danubian ship traffic.

In the 11th century a burial chapel for St Gellért was erected, the first sanctuary on the site of the Belvárosi plébánia-templom (Inner City Parish Church, *see p54)*. The unfortunate missionary had in fact been about to cross from the Buda side when he was intercepted and drowned in the river by supporters of the pagan faction (1046).

Shortly afterwards (1061), the first documentary mention of the town of Pest appears.

Medieval and Baroque Pest

In the 11th and 12th centuries, Pest expanded to become a substantial and wealthy trading town, with a royal residence, a Dominican cloister, and a parish church. After the Tartar invasion of 1241, King Béla IV renewed its privileges as a Royal Free Town, but many of its mainly German inhabitants moved to the comparative safety of Buda. In the 14th century, it boomed again under the Anjou dynasty, when the parish church was enlarged and altered to the form of a *hallenkirche* (hall church).

After the Turkish occupation (1541–1686), building began again in Pest; a hospital for war veterans was built by Italian architects in 1716, together with several Baroque convents

Poet Attila József sculpted in brooding pose

and churches (for example, those of the Servites, the Franciscans, and the Hungarian order of Paulites). Of the Baroque palaces built by aristocrats, few traces remain; Andreas Mayerhoffer's Péterffy Palace (1755) in Pesti Barnabás utca (now the Százéves restaurant) is a rare example.

Expansion

Pest came into its own in the 19th century. In 1805 János Hild presented his plans to improve the city to the Embellishment Commission supported by the Palatine. The proposed parks and public buildings were to be financed by selling building plots and by the revenues of customs and local taxes. The inner city (Belváros) thereafter became a largely residential area with churches and schools. Neighbouring Lipótváros (Leopold's Town) was the business centre, increasingly also the domain of wealthy assimilated Jews. Neo-Classical buildings – the Magyar Nemzeti Múzeum (National Museum), the

Calvinist and Lutheran churches – gave the city its monumental character up to the revolution against the Habsburgs of 1848, when many Neo-Classical dwellings were destroyed.

In the second half of the 19th century, Pest became the hub of a rapidly expanding and industrialising capital. Whereas in 1850 the populations of Buda and Pest were roughly equal, by 1900 only one in six Budapestians lived in Buda. The great boulevards crossed by the radial of Andrássy út were now built, as were three new bridges. Miklós Ybl located magnificent Neo-Renaissance palaces along the streets and designed a graceful opera house (1884). Theatres, museums, and hotels, many on a grand scale, enriched the cityscape of Pest. The monumental Szent István bazilika (St Stephen's Basilica) was begun in 1851 and the even more grandiose Országház (Parliament) was completed just after the turn of the century. The Millennial Celebrations of 1896 put the seal on all this dynamism and self-confidence, while the idiosyncratic buildings of Ödön Lechner (*see pp68–9*) and his school gave expression to the Magyar soul in architecture.

From the 20th century onwards, Pest has begun to sprawl into suburbia, but at its heart is still the bustle and business of that dynamic 19th-century city, now reawakening to capitalistic enterprise, artistic creativity, and gourmet refinement.

The Parliament (Országház) as seen from Buda

THE ANCIENT TOWN OF ÓBUDA

The Roman province of Pannonia was created in the first century BC and divided by Trajan into Upper and Lower Pannonia around AD 106. Aquincum (*see pp94–5*) was the civil capital of Lower Pannonia. Close to it was the military *castrum* (camp), at the Óbuda end of Árpád híd/Árpád Bridge, and its associated domestic buildings known as *canabae*.

Two of the chiefs of the seven Magyar tribes (Kende and Kurszán) took up residence in Óbuda, and the first church – a burial chapel built over the grave of the paramount chief, Árpád – was raised in Óbuda at the end of the 10th or the beginning of the 11th century.

In the Middle Ages, the town increased in wealth and importance, particularly under Béla III, who entertained Frederick Barbarossa here in 1189. A Cistercian cloister was built, and other religious orders followed in the 14th century, when the widowed queen of King Charles Robert of Anjou moved her palace to the town. Under Sigismund of Luxembourg, Óbuda even boasted a university (founded in 1389, the first in Hungary).

Like Buda and Pest, the town suffered under the Turkish occupation, but in the 18th century the Habsburgs bestowed the

Fő tér in Óbuda

Óbuda lands on the Zichy family. They built their great mansion close to Fő tér (*see p35*), and encouraged Jews to settle, thus boosting the area's economy. Crafts and trade received further stimulus in the 19th century when Count Széchenyi founded the shipyard on Óbuda Island and the Goldberger textile factory began operations (both still exist).

Sadly, Óbuda has suffered from the ravages of time and Communism. The once picturesque provincial town is now a concrete jungle with a few isolated pockets of Baroque charm and elegance. A visit to these relics (and the delightful local museum at Kiscelli) will give a hint of past glories.

A surviving capital at Aquincum

The Royal Palace as viewed from the Gellért Monument

Walk: Szabadság híd to Ferenciek tere

This is one of two walks exploring the historic core of Pest. It begins just outside the former old city wall (follow the route in green on the map below).

Allow about an hour.

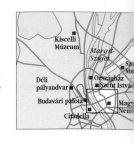

Start at the Pest side of Szabadság híd (see p41).

1 Közgazdaság Tudományi Egyetem (University of Economics)

The former Karl Marx University at

Fővám tér 8 was one of the more liberal institutions under Communism. Miklós Ybl's building (1874) was originally the Customs House. Its grandeur reflects Pest's importance as a centre of Danubian trade in the late-19th century.

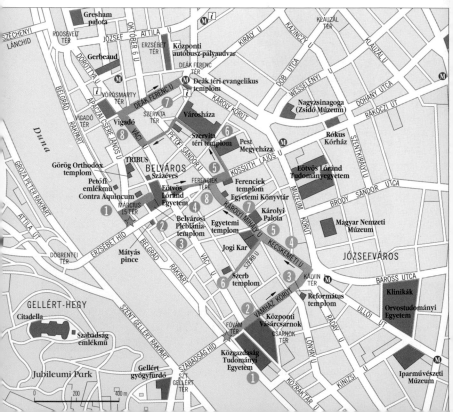

2 Központi Vásárcsarnok (Central Market)

Behind the university is the largest of Pest's five market halls (*see p145*), opened in 1897 as a spin-off from the 1896 Millennial Celebrations.
Walk east along Vámház körút as far as Kálvin tér.

3 Református Templom (Calvinist Church)

This rather plain Neo-Classical church (*see p56*) took 14 years to build in the early 19th century due to funding problems. It achieved its present form in 1859. Inside is the tomb of Countess Zichy (who was Anglican by faith). The Calvinist College at nearby Ráday utca 28 has an interesting display of bibles (enquire at the entrance).
From Kálvin tér it is a few minutes' walk on Múzeum körút to the Magyar Nemzeti Múzeum (Hungarian National Museum, see pp74–5). Otherwise turn left into Kecskeméti utca.

4 The Old City Wall

The post-modern Hotel Korona, with a bridge section overarching the road, stands on the site of the city gate. Just beyond the archway is an inscription on the wall: '*Itt állt a középkori pesti városfal*' ('Here stood the medieval city wall of Pest').

5 Jogi Kar and Egyetemi Templom (Faculty of Law and University Church)

Further along the street on your left is the elegant Neo-Baroque Faculty of Law and adjoining it the University Church (1742, *see pp54–5*), probably the work of Andreas Mayerhoffer. In the early-19th century it was a centre of the reform movement. A school for nurturing and promoting the Hungarian language (in opposition to German) was founded here in 1831.
Turn left down Szerb utca.

6 Szerb Templom (Serbian Church)

You now come to the pretty Serbian Church (*see p57*) built by the Serbian community in 1698. It is said that at the beginning of the 19th century every fourth house in Pest was owned by a Serb merchant.
Retrace your steps to Károlyi Mihály utca.

7 Károlyi Palota (Károlyi Palace)

Károlyi Mihály utca 16 was the city residence of Count Mihály Károlyi, first president of the Hungarian Republic in 1918. His widow, known as the 'red countess', kept an apartment here towards the end of her life. Mayerhoffer's Baroque palace was given its Neo-Classical aspect in 1799.

8 Egyetemi Könyvtár (University Library)

At the end of Károlyi Mihály utca is the south side of Ferenciek tere (Square of the Franciscans). At No. 10 is the freshly restored University Library, an impressive Neo-Renaissance building (1876). There are frescoes in the reading room by Károly Lotz and Mór Than. Notable are the eleven codices from the great library of King Matthias Corvinus that are kept here.
Buses leave from Ferenciek tere for various destinations and there is also a metro stop for the blue line.

Walk: Erzsébet híd to Deák Ferenc tér

The walk begins at the Roman fort where Pest originated, and includes the fashionable shopping area of Váci utca. See map on page 30, following the route in orange.
Allow 1 hour.

Start in front of the church at Március 15 tér at the Pest end of Erzsébet híd (see pp40–41).

1 Contra Aquincum
This diminutive fortress (*see p94*), with walls 3m thick, was a 4th-century outpost in barbarian territory that protected the main town of Aquincum on the far side of the river.

2 Mátyás Pince
If you want to experience a typical (if touristy) Hungarian restaurant with gypsy music, cross under the bridge to the Mátyás pince at Március 15 tér 7, an institution since it opened in 1904.

A bookshop in fashionable Váci utca

3 Belvárosi Plébániatemplom (Inner City Parish Church)
The most historic church of Pest (*see p54*) is on Március 15 tér. It has had an eventful history: the Romanesque and Gothic churches were both largely destroyed, while the Turks turned the diminished building into a mosque. Highlights of the mostly Baroque interior are the two lovely Renaissance tabernacles made of red marble.
A detour to the north takes you to the Görög Orthodox templom (Greek Orthodox Church) at Petőfi tér 2 (drop in to hear the singing at 6pm on Saturdays).

4 Eötvös Lóránd Egyetem (Lóránd Eötvös University)
Named after the distinguished physicist (1848–1919), this is Budapest's main university and was originally a Piarist 'gymnasium' (secondary school). You pass under the building's connecting archway on your way to Kigyó utca and thence to Ferenciek tere. In the parallel Pesti Barnabás utca, at No. 2, is the Százéves (100 Years) restaurant, located in one of the few remaining Baroque palaces of Pest.

5 Párizsi Udvar (Paris Arcade)
Flanking Ferenciek tere to the north is

he striking Jugendstil (Art Nouveau)
rcade designed by Henrik Schmahl
1911), with its oriental-looking stained-
;lass cupola. There is a good bookshop
iere, a newsagent with foreign
iewspapers, and the popular Piccolo
)ar. Jégbüfé, on Ferenciek tere, is a good
)lace to stop for light refreshments
)efore carring on across Kossuth Lajos
ıtca to the Ferenciek templom
Ferenciek church, *see p55*). On the
iorth wall is a relief showing Count
Wesselényi rescuing Pest inhabitants by
)oat during the floods of 1838.
*Take the next street left after Petőfi
Sándor utca.*

5 Pest Megyeháza, Városháza
(County and City Halls)

The Pest County Hall (No. 7 Városház
ıtca) is a simple Neo-Classical building
1830), while the City Hall (Nos 9–11) is
ın elegant Baroque structure designed
)y Antonio Martinelli in 1735 as a
iospital for the war-wounded. It was
established by Emperor Charles VI. An
ımposing Atlas bearing a globe stands
)ver the entrance.

7 Szervita Tér (Servite Square)

The street leads to the square which was
recently renamed after the Servite Order,
whose church (1725) stands on the
corner (*see p57*). Two fine Jugendstil
houses (*see pp70–71*) at Nos 3 and 5 are
worth a glance, especially the mosaic in
the gable of No. 3, which is a florid
representation of 'The Transfiguration
of Hungary'.
*Turn left into Petőfi Sándor utca, right
immediately into Régiposta utca, then
right again into Váci utca.*

The statue of Vörösmarty, rich in detail

8 Váci Utca to Vörösmarty Tér/Gerbeaud Cukrászda (Coffee House)

This fashionable shopping area (a
pedestrian zone) is always bustling with
people. On the square is the monument
to the poet Mihály Vörösmarty
(1800–55). At the north end is the
celebrated 1870 Gerbeaud coffee house
and confectioner's, with its enticing
menu of Viennese and Hungarian
pastries (*see p170*).
*The metro junction, where the three lines
meet, is located nearby at Deák Ferenc tér
to the east.*

Walk: Óbuda

High-rise blocks have ruined this once delightful area, but there are still a few pockets of historic interest and charm that make this a lovely walk.

Allow 2 hours, or 3 hours if the Kiscelli Múzeum is included.

Take bus No. 86 from Batthyány tér to Nagyszombat utca, or the HÉV railway to Tímár utca, and walk back south.

1 Amfiteátrum

This vast Roman arena was built for the military in the 2nd century and could accommodate 15,000 spectators. According to the medieval German epic

Das Nibelungenlied, Attila the Hun ruled in the 5th century from 'Etzilburg', sometimes identified with this amphitheatre.

A longish detour via Nagyszombat utca and Bécsi út is required for the Kiscelli Museum (*see p73*), housed in a former Trinitarian monastery on top of the hill.

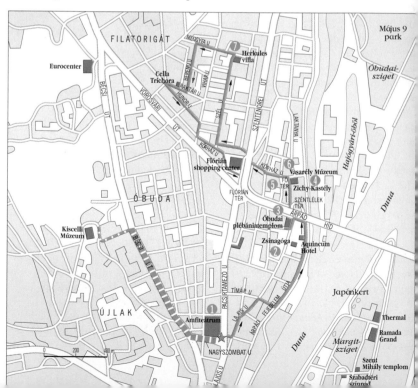

*Bear right along Lajos utca and right
again along Tímár utca. You emerge on a
green sward bordered by Lajos utca and
Árpád fejedelem útja.*

2 Zsinagóga

The fine Neo-Classical building of this
former synagogue at Lajos utca 163, was
designed by András Landherr in 1825
for the growing Jewish community,
many of whom were involved in the
area's silk and leather industries. The
synagogue is now a television studio;
just beyond it is the new Hotel
Aquincum, an especially pleasing brick
and glass construction.

3 Óbudai Plébániatemplom (Óbuda Parish Church)

In front of the church (*see p55*) is a lawn
and chestnut avenue lined with
sandstone statues. It stands on the site of
the Roman military camp, part of which
has been excavated. The tomb of Count
Peter Zichy, who was given the lands of
Óbuda by the king, following the
expulsion of the Turks, lies beneath the
pulpit inside the church. Just beyond is
the Calvinist Church in Kálvin köz,
notable for its presbytery (Károly Kós,
1909) in Transylvanian vernacular style.
*Cross under Árpád Bridge to Szentlélek
tér and Fő tér. In the passageway are the
remains of the Roman military baths.*

4 Zichy-Kastély (Zichy Mansion)

The Baroque family home of the Zichys
was built in 1757 by Henrik Jäger. It
contains the Lajos Kassák Memorial
Rooms, dedicated to Hungary's greatest
avant-garde artist and writer. Adjoining
it is the Vasarely Museum with work by

the founder of 'Op Art', Hungarian-born
Viktor Vasarely.

5 Fő Tér

The delightful main square of Óbuda is
flanked by Baroque houses, several of
them traditional Hungarian bistros. At
No. 4 is a collection of folk artefacts and
at No. 4 the Óbudai Múzeum.

6 Imre Varga's Sculpture

At the corner of Laktanya utca is
Strollers in the Rain, Imre Varga's
amusing sculpture of bronze ladies with
umbrellas. More of his work may be
seen at No. 7.
*Pass beneath Szentendrei út and bear
right to the Herkules Villa.*

7 Herkules Villa

The Herkules Villa, at Meggyfa utca 21,
evidently belonged to a well-to-do
Roman. From the same period are the
remains of a rare *cella trichora* (clover-
leaf chapel) at the junction of Hunor
utca and Raktár utca. (*See also p95*.)
*Continue to Flórián tér, from where trams
run to Pest, or return to Szentlélek tér, for
buses to Buda and Pest.*

Zichy Mansion (Kassák Múzeum)
*Tel: (06 1) 368 7021. Open: Tue–Sun 10am–
6pm, 5pm in winter.* The Zichy Mansion also
houses the **Óbudai Museum** *(tel: (06 1)
388 2534), www.extra.hu/obmuzeum*
Open Tue–Sun 10am–6pm.
Vasarely Museum *Tel: (06 1) 250 1540.
Open: Tue–Sun 10am–6pm, 5pm in winter.*
Zsigmond Kun Collection (Lakasmúzeum)
*Tel: (06 1) 386 1138. Open: Tue–Fri 2–6pm,
Sat–Sun 10am–6pm.*
Imre Varga Collection *Tel: (06 1) 250 0274.
Open: Tue–Sun 10am–5.30pm.*

BATHS OF BUDA AND PEST

Of Budapest's many public baths, the four described here all have good facilities, interesting historical features, and architectural charm.

Gellért Gyógyfürdő (Gellért Spa)

The Buda spa most popular with visitors is where the earliest inhabitants exploited the mineral springs of the Gellért Hill; later a local hermit worked miracles with the water; and later still, the poor of Buda bathed here (and watered their horses) during the Turkish occupation.

The present establishment goes back to a decision of the City Council in 1901 to purchase the land and exploit the springs, whose outlet had been covered over when the Szabadság híd (Freedom Bridge) was built in 1896. Plans for a hotel and spa were finally approved in 1909. By the summer of 1914, only the walls had been built, but, despite the war, the building was completed and opened in 1918.

The architecture is in an agreeably over-the-top version of Jugendstil. The main indoor pool (with jets of bubbles pumped from the floor for 10 minutes each hour) presents a fantasia of mosaics, columns, and gushing gargoyles. The entrance hall recalls the grandiosity of the Caracalla Baths in Rome, while frivolity is catered for in the 'wave-bath' in the ornamental terraced gardens at the rear.

Kelenhegyi út 2–4. Tel: (06 1) 466 6166. Open: Oct–May, Mon–Fri 6am–6pm, Sat–Sun 6am–4pm; May–Sep, Mon–Fri 6am–7pm, Sat–Sun 6am–7pm (pool), 6am–5pm (spa); Jul & Aug, Fri & Sat 8pm–midnight (with music). Trams: 47, 49 (from Pest), 18, 19 (from Buda).

The wave bath of Buda's most popular spa, the Gellért

Király Gyógyfürdő (King Spa)

The bath, built by Pasha Mustapha Sokollu, was completed in 1578. There was no thermal spring nearby, so water was piped from the Lukács area. The ground-plan of the bath is a rectangle, on which has been built an octagonal basin. Ovehead arches a cupola studded with tiny hexagonal light wells.

The bath had several owners after the reconquest of 1686, the last (1796) being a certain Ferenc König (Király in Hungarian), from whom it takes its name. The charming Neo-Classical wing was added in 1826.

Fő utca 84. Tel: (06 1) 202 3688. Open: for women, Tue, Thu & Sat 7am–5pm; for men, Mon, Wed & Fri 9am–7pm. Closed: Sun. Admission charge. Metro: to Batthyány tér.

Lukács Gyógy-és Strandfürdő (St Luke Spa)

Under the Turks, the spring here was used to drive a gunpowder mill, although a hospital spa named after St Luke had occupied the site of the present baths in the Middle Ages. Baths were once more in operation by the 1850s, enlarged in 1863, and again in 1884 when the powder mill was finally discontinued.

Lukács is an oasis of calm and charm with its huge courtyard in the shade of ancient plane-trees. The clientele is intellectual and professional, and gossip as important an activity here as bathing.

Frankel Leó út 25–29. Tel: (06 1) 326 1695. Open: Mon–Fri 6am–7pm, Sat & Sun 6am–5pm. Admission charge. Tram: 17 (from Buda).

Széchenyi Spa

Széchenyi Gyórgyfürdő (Széchenyi Spa)

The most impressive spa on the Pest side, named after Count István Széchenyi, opened in 1913 (enlarged in 1927). It is a rambling Neo-Baroque establishment supplied by a thermal spring discovered in 1876. The water rises from a depth of 1,256m at a temperature of 70°C.

Állatkerti körút 11 (in Városliget). Tel: (06 1) 363 3210. Open: daily 6am–7pm (last entry 6pm). Admission charge (deposit system, part of it returned depending on length of stay, keep receipt carefully). Metro: to Széchenyi Fürdő.

Smaller Baths
Two thermal baths from the Turkish era are: **Rácfürdő** Hadnagy utca. *Tel: (06 1) 356 1322*; and **Rüdafürdő** Doboenter tér 9. *Tel: (06 1) 356 110.*

Spa City

In the prehistory of Buda, hundreds of spring-fed streams trickled off the hills into a riparian swamp, and thence into the Danube. When the Celtic Eravisci arrived, they occupied the Gellért Hill and, probably, other parts of the west bank. When the Romans took over they retained the picturesque name the Celts had given to their settlement – Ak-Ink, meaning 'Abundant Waters' – and Latinised it to Aquincum.

There is still a Római fürdő (Roman bath) near the ruins of Aquincum, one of three

fed by a source at nearby Csillaghegy. It seems that the Magyars, too, exploited the waters, for the newcomers divided Buda into areas known as Felsőhévíz (Upper Thermal Waters) and Alsóhévíz (Lower Thermal Waters).

In the Middle Ages, at least two hospitals based on spas were founded

(at today's Gellért and Lukács baths) by the Knights Hospitallers of St John. For the Turks, bathing had a ritual significance; between 1541 and 1686 numerous Turkish baths were built, that remain today as almost the sole architectural and cultural legacy of Ottoman rule.

Budapest was officially designated a spa city in 1934 by the International Spa Congress (which subsequently moved its headquarters to the city). It certainly deserves the title, for there are 123 springs in Buda, Óbuda, and Pest, spouting an estimated 70 million litres of water daily and supplying 47 baths, of which 12 have extensive medical facilities. The water temperature varies between 24° and 78°C. Many of the springs are sulphurous or slightly radioactive: they are used to treat rheumatism, circulation

disorders, and gynaecological complaints.

Budapest baths have something for everybody: there are open-air and sports pools, artificial wave baths and bubble baths, medicinal and mud baths, warm, cool, and Turkish baths. All those pounds put on from consumption of heavy Magyar dishes can (theoretically) be lost again in the city's 'abundant waters'.

The spas of Buda and Pest evoke memories of a leisured age

Bridges

In 1870, when Gusztáv Zsigmondy was carrying out a regulation of the Danube, he discovered, just north of today's Árpád Bridge, the sunken piles of a wooden Roman bridge. This was the first and only Budapest bridge until the 19th century (*see pp100–101*).

Building the Elizabeth Bridge greatly altered the landscape on the Pest side

Although Sigismund of Luxembourg and Matthias Corvinus seem to have planned stone bridges in the 15th century, nothing came of their projects. A pontoon was in operation by the beginning of the 16th century; Turkish engineers subsequently built a more sophisticated 70-drum version, roughly where the Elizabeth Bridge is now.

After the reconquest, an ingenious so-called 'flying bridge' was put into operation by the enterprising Viennese. It consisted of a catamaran that was attached to the banks by long ropes resting on barges. By manipulating the rudder, the boat could be made to swing from shore to shore, using the force of the current. It was in use until 1790, by which time an elegant 'swaying prom-enade' with 43 pontoons, had been built. Opened at dawn and midday, it had to be dismantled in winter because of ice-floes. The municipal authorities would bed safe paths across the ice with straw, charging users double the pontoon toll (nobles, soldiers, and students went free). During a big freeze, fairs and balls would be held on the river. The last ball (in 1883) ended in tragedy when the ice suddenly gave way, tipping the dance floor into the glacial waters and drowning 40 people.

Building and Naming Bridges

Since the first of Budapest's bridges in modern times was completed in 1848, nine more have been built within the city boundaries to relieve traffic congestion in the centre. The vicissitudes of history are reflected in the various name changes: today's 'Liberty Bridge' was planned as 'Customs House Square Bridge', but inaugurated by the emperor himself as 'Franz Joseph Bridge'. The 'Chain Bridge' later became 'Széchenyi Chain Bridge' in honour of its originator, while 'Petőfi Bridge', to the south, bore the name of the inter-war regent Miklós Horthy for a while.

The Árpád Bridge to the north was officially 'Stalin Bridge' in the 1950s, and reverted to its original name after the 1956 revolution. All Budapest's bridges had to be rebuilt after the war, as they were blown up by the retreating Germans.

Erzsébet Híd (Elizabeth Bridge)

The 290-m suspension bridge was built between 1897 and 1903 and reconstructed to a modern design after World War I. Its structure weighs just over 1,000 tonnes, but carries 29 90-tonne components of carriageway. Building it entailed wholesale

destruction of the medieval core of Pest – the Old Town Hall was demolished and the Inner City Parish Church only escaped thanks to vociferous popular protest.
Buses: 5, 7, 7A, 8, 78 & 112.

Margit Híd (Margaret Bridge)

A French engineer, Ernest Gouin, designed the second bridge to be built (1876) after the Chain Bridge (*see pp100–101*). To keep its two sections vertical to the current (divided here by Margaret Island) there is a 30-degree angle at the apex. A supplementary ramp (1900) leads down to the island.
Trams: 4, 6; buses: 6, 26, 91 & 191.

Szabadság Híd (Freedom Bridge)

An all-Hungarian effort in design and construction, this iron console bridge was inaugurated by Emperor Franz Joseph in 1896. The silver spike he ceremonially struck into the Pest abutment was stolen during the 1956 revolution. The Hungarian coat of arms is displayed on the central arches, topped by the mythic turul bird, supposed begetter of the Árpád dynasty.
Trams: 47 & 49.

Freedom Bridge (formerly Franz Joseph Bridge)

Walk: Tabán and Gellért-hegy

On this walk the self-confident architectural elegance of the 19th century is interspersed with glimpses of a turbulent past.

Allow 2 hours.

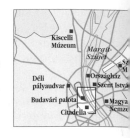

Begin at Clark Ádám tér, reached by buses 16 from Pest or 86 along Fő utca on the Buda side.

1 Clark Ádám Tér

The square, situated at the western end of the Széchenyi Lánchíd (Chain Bridge, *see pp100–101*), is named after the bridge's Scottish builder. The northern side is flanked by two fine blocks made by Miklós Ybl (1814–91). To the west is the road tunnel under Castle Hill, also built by Clark. In front of the funicular railway (*sikló*) up to the castle is the modern kilometre stone, whence all distances from the capital are measured.

Walk 100m along the Lánchíd utca.
On your right you come to the Várbazár.

2 Várbazár

This once elegant, now decayed, complex of steps and terraces was designed by Miklós Ybl to link the castle with the Danube shore. Across the street is a statue of Ybl in front of the 'Kiosk' (now a casino), which he built in Neo-Renaissance style to camouflage the castle's water-pumping station.

3 Semmelweis Orvostörténeti Múzeum (Semmelweis Museum of Medicine)

At Apród utca 1–3 is the Neo-Classical house of the Museum of Medicine (*see p78*), named after the discoverer of puerperal fever, who was born here. József Antall, prime minister from 1990 to 1993, was once director.

4 Török Sírok (Turkish Graves)

Take the steps leading up between the museum and another Ybl-designed house where Adam Clark died. At the top follow the path round to the right. Under a locust tree are some lonely Turkish gravestones with inscriptions. *From here walk back southwards, passing the Arany Szarvas Étterem (The Golden Stag) restaurant in a simple Baroque building on your right.*

5 Tabáni Plébániatemplom (Tabán Parish Church)

The Tabán was a lively area of pubs and traders until its demolition in 1930. The parish church of St Catherine survives at Attila út 11. Many of the Tabán's inhabitants were Serbs, hence the name Rác fürdő (Serbian baths) of the establishment southwest of the church across the road junction.

6 Erzsébet Királynö Szobra (Statue of Queen Elizabeth)

South of the church under the Elizabeth Bridge's feeder roads is the monument to Emperor Franz Joseph's wife, the pro-Hungarian Elizabeth of Bavaria. A plaque recalls that the previous monument on this site, to the pro-Fascist politician Gyula Gömbös, was blown up by the Communist resistance in 1944. *Make your way under the spaghetti junction to the steps at the foot of the Gellért Hill.*

7 Gellért Emlékmű (Gellért Monument)

A winding stairway leads to this memorial (*see p97*) to the missionary St Gellért (Gerard of Csanád), allegedly martyred here. There is also a scenic waterfall here that adds to the ambience.

8 Szabadság Emlékmű (Freedom Monument)

The steep climb to the top of the hill is rewarded with stunning views. On the summit is the Freedom Monument (*see p98*) put up at the end of the war by the Russians. The heroic Russian soldiers have been removed, leaving only an allegorical female figure.

9 Citadella (Citadel)

Above the monument is the Citadella, built by the Austrians in 1854 as barracks and fortress from which to keep a vigil on the unruly inhabitants of Budapest. It now has shops, a restaurant, small hotel, and viewing terrace. *Descend through a pleasant park to the Gellért spa (gyógy-fürdő) and the buses and trams on Gellért tér.*

Statue of Queen Elizabeth

Walk: Margit Sziget

Margaret Island is Budapest's loveliest park, with a history stretching back to Roman times. Originally it was three islands, the largest of which (Rabbit Island) was for long a royal hunting estate. Margaret was the daughter of King Béla IV. She retreated to a convent here in 1252, when only nine years old.

Allow 1½ hours.

The walk begins at the southern end of the island, reached by bus 26 from the east side of Margit híd (Margaret Bridge). Alight at the first stop on the island.

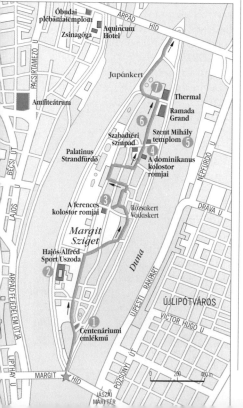

1 Centenáriumi Emlékmű (Centennial Monument)

The large fountain, colourfully lit at night, was erected in 1972. It commemorates the centenary of the unification of Buda, Pest, and Óbuda in 1872–3.

2 Hajós-Alfréd Sport Uszoda and Palatinus Strandfürdő

Serious swimmers can enjoy the massive indoor pool of the Hajós Baths, named after the gold medallist at the Athens (1896) Olympics. Hajós was also a successful architect and designed the pool and the building in 1930. On the way to the Palatinus open-air baths (which have a mechanism for making artificial waves), you pass the attractive Rózsakert (Rose Garden) on your right.

3 Ferences Kolostor Romjai

Between the baths is a ruined Franciscan church dating from 1272. Palatine Joseph's splendid villa built next to the chapel in 1796 was destroyed in the 1838 flood. The Archduke encouraged development of the island's spa and laid out gardens, but the public were not allowed in until 1869.

4 Dominikánus Kolostor Romjai/Szabadtéri Színpad

Northeast of the Palatinus Baths are the ruins of the Dominican convent where St Margaret lived a life of daunting asceticism (even washing was viewed with suspicion). Not far to the west is a water tower and the open-air stage used for opera performances in summer.

5 Szent Mihály Templom (St Michael's Church)

To the northeast is the reconstructed Romanesque church of St Michael, built in 1930 using materials from the original 12th-century Premonstra-tensian church (the ruins of the Premonstratensian convent are nearby). In the church is a 15th-century bell, discovered in 1914 under a tree that had

St Michael's Church

blown down in a storm. The monks had probably buried it before the arrival of the Turks to prevent it being melted down to make cannons.

6 Sculpture Avenue

Along the promenade to the Grand Hotel are busts of Hungary's greatest painters, poets, and musicians. Among them is one of the 19th-century poet János Arany, who liked to sit under the island's trees in the evening composing his romantic lyrics.

7 Ramada Grand Hotel, Hotel Thermal

Further north is the beautifully restored Grand Hotel designed by Miklós Ybl, a true reflection of a more leisurely age. Beyond it is the ugly Hotel Thermal; to the west the charming Japanese Garden. *At the northern end of the island, bus 26, which has a circular route, can be boarded again. Otherwise climb Árpád híd for bus 106 to Óbuda-Aquincum or Árpád híd metro (Pest side).*

Open-air theatre on Margaret Island

Walk: Rózsadomb and Víziváros

At the turn of the 20th century, elegant villas were built on the Rózsadomb (Hill of Roses), while the Víziváros (Water Town), so-called for being constantly flooded, was settled by craftsmen and fishermen in the Middle Ages.

Allow 2½ hours.

Start from the western end of the Margaret Bridge (Margit híd) and make your way to Frankel Leó út via Vidra utca.

1 Lukács Gyogy-és-Strandfürdő and Málom-Tó

At Frankel Leó út 25–7 is the Lukács spa (*see p37*) with a pleasant tree-shaded courtyard. On the wall are plaques erected by grateful beneficiaries of the healing waters. Across the street is a ruined Turkish gunpowder mill and a millpond (Málom-tó). If you walk through to the back of Lukács and turn left, you can see through a window the Turkish 'Császár Bath', built by Pasha Sokollu in 1570.

Turn up a cobbled street at the junction of Török utca and Frankel Leó út. Turn left before No. 22.

2 Gül Baba Türbéje

This tomb of a famous Dervish scholar (*see p60*) is reputedly the northernmost Muslim shrine in Europe. It is customary to remove your shoes before entering.

Climb up to the junction of Gül Baba utca and Vérhalom utca. Make your way down Apostol utca to Rómer Flóris utca, across Margit körút and along Fekete Sas utca.

3 Bem Szobor (József Bem Monument)

The Polish general Bem fought for the

Hungarians in the 1848 War of Independence. The statue represents him urging on his troops.

4 Flórián Kápolna

The Baroque chapel of St Florian (1760) is nearby at Fő utca 90; peer through the glass entrance to see the frescoes and a finely carved pulpit. St Florian's has belonged to the Greek Catholics since 1920.

5 Király Gyógyfürdő

These baths (*see p37*) were built for the garrison under the Turkish occupation. In the dimly lit interior the play of light beams in the rising steam is an aesthetic experience. The baths are a centre of the Budapest gay scene.

6 Öntödei Múzeum (Foundry Museum)

A sign next to the baths points to this unusual museum. The exhibits deal with metal working from the Bronze Age to that of steel. Note the romantic statue of the engineer Abraham Ganz.
Continue south on Fő utca past the grim military prison (Nos 70–74), and the Nagy Imre tér.

7 Batthyány Tér

The Szent Erzsébet templom (Church of the Elizabethan Nuns) is on your left, just before you reach the square. Their charitable tradition is maintained in the old people's home now occupying their convent. Immediately on the right is the Rococo inn, At the Sign of the White Cross, behind which the post-chaise used to leave for Vienna. Szent Anna templom (St Anne's Church, *see p56*) is

to the south. Next to it is the Angelika coffee-house, sometimes described as the favourite rendezvous for the 'society of old hens'.

8 Batthyány Tér to Clark Ádám Tér

Further along Fő utca is the Szilágyi Dezső teri templom (Calvinist Church) designed by Samu Pecz, whose statue stands beside it. Beyond it is the former Capuchin Church (No. 32), remodelled in the 19th century. Opposite the Neo-Classical No. 20 is the graceful Post-Modern Francia Kultúra Intézete (French Institute, built in 1992).
Buses for Pest and Buda leave from Clark Ádám tér nearby.

Öntödei Múzeum
Bem József utca 20. *Tel: (06 1) 201 4370.*
Open: Tue–Sun 9am–5pm.

Statue of General Bem

Budavári Palota

Royal Palace

Following the devastating Tartar invasions of 1240–41, King Béla IV decided to fortify the southern part of the Buda plateau, since the 11th century a defenceless agrarian settlement and part of 'Minor Pesth' (Lesser Pest).

The Matthias Fountain on Castle Hill

The castle remained modest until Louis the Great of Anjou moved his court here from Visegrád, probably in 1347. His successor, Sigismund of Luxembourg (1387–1437), built a new L-shaped palace known as the 'Friss Palota' (New Palace). An indefatigable traveller, Sigismund, son of Charles IV of Bohemia, scoured the courts of Europe for first-rate craftsmen whom he could lure to Buda. It was under Sigismund that various engineering projects were undertaken, including the building of a horse-driven pump to supply the palace with Danube water. He was also responsible for placing the vast chain across the river so as to enforce the city's staple rights that before merchants went elsewhere, they should give the people of the city a chance to buy their goods and thus earn an income for the city.

The Golden Age

The golden age of the court at Buda was that of King Matthias Corvinus (1458–90): his chapel was equipped with a water organ and his marvellous Bibliotheca Corviniana had 2,000 illuminated codices fastened to lecterns with golden chains. An army of craftsmen made beautiful ceramic stoves for the winter quarters, carved marble fireplaces and doorways, and gilded the coffered ceilings of sleeping chambers. Foreigners were duly impressed. An Italian wrote: 'In all Europe the three most beautiful cities are Venice on the sea, Buda on the hill, and Florence on the plain.' Matthias's chief architect (resident in Buda between 1479 and 1491) was in fact a Florentine, Chimenti Camicia; another great contemporary architect, Giovanni Dalmata (a

PALACE APPROACH

The Royal Palace can be approached from Szarvas tér in the south, reached by buses 86 (Buda side) and 5 or 78 (from Pest). Leaving the Southern Rondella on your right, you pass through the Ferdinand Gate, close to the menacing Mace Tower. Access to the entrance to the Budapest History Museum is via walled gardens.

From the north the palace may be reached using the *sikló* (funicular) from Clark Ádám tér, by bus 16 from Pest (Erzsébet tér, Deák F tér metro), or by taking the *várbusz* (minibus) from Moszkva tér to Szent György tér.

Dalmatian of Italian stock and builder of the magnificent cathedral of Sibenik), also worked for Europe's most glittering and ambitious monarch.

Decay and Revival

During the 145-year-long Turkish occupation (1541–1686) the palace fell into decay. In 1678, lightning struck the gunpowder store, causing an explosion that destroyed most of Sigismund's palace. After the reconquest of Hungary by the Habsburgs and their allies, Charles VI's and Maria Theresa's architects razed much of the Gothic and Renaissance remnants and built a small Baroque palace. No longer used as a royal residence – at different times it housed a convent and a university – it

was eventually turned over to the Austrian Palatine (Viceroy) in 1790.

After being damaged in the 1848 War of Independence, the palace enjoyed its last flowering after the Compromise with Austria of 1867. Miklós Ybl, then Alajos Hauszmann, altered and considerably enlarged the Baroque structure between 1869 and 1905. During the inter-war period, the so-called Regent of Hungary, Admiral Horthy, installed himself here. In the closing days of World War II, the whole place was reduced to rubble by the Russian bombardment. Though it has since been rebuilt incorporating some relics of the earlier palaces, it lacks the grace and splendour of its illustrious predecessors.

The Lion Gate and rear courtyard of the Royal Palace complex, rebuilt after total devastation in World War II

Budapesti Történeti Múzeum (Historical Museum of the City of Budapest)

Remnants of the Old Palace

Descend the stairway from the ticket office for a tour through the layers of the Renaissance and Gothic castle. At the entrance are the coats of arms of the Árpáds, the Anjous, Matthias Corvinus, and the Jagiellon dynasties.

Highlights of the tour include the Renaissance Hall, with a fragment of coffered ceiling in red marble by Giovanni Dalmata, an imposing marble fireplace, and elegant reliefs of King Matthias and Queen Beatrice. You will also pass an ice-pit connected to the hanging garden above by a chute, and an area where the cistern was located.

Further on are the former Queen's Quarters and the Royal Chapel of 1380 (the chapel's lower part was rededicated on 18 August 1990 as St Stephen's Chapel). Walking on from here you will come to the large, spacious, partly Renaissance hall, where concerts are sometimes organised.

Gothic Statues from the Royal Palace

Along the corridor from the ticket counter, a special display has been created for the beautiful Gothic statues

The rich collection of Late-Gothic triptychs in the Hungarian National Gallery

unearthed during excavations in 1974. They were made during the reign of Sigismund of Luxembourg and appear to have been thrown into a builder's trench for use as rubble. Exactly why this happened is still a puzzle – perhaps the plans for the palace changed before they could be installed; or perhaps Sigismund's notoriously spendthrift ways finally caught up with him and unpaid workers indulged in a little iconoclasm.

The statues are dated to the third decade of the 15th century and fall into two categories, profane and sacred. Of the profane, some have lean elegant features, and could be members of the Anjou dynasty with their ladies, and contemporary knights and bishops. Others in this category are fore-

A Gothic statue discovered in the Royal Palace

shortened, suggesting that they were placed high up; they have rounder, more typically Magyar features. Figures in the sacred series have been identified as apostles or prophets.

The striking quality of these works is eloquent testimony to the wealth of Buda in the late Middle Ages, which could afford to employ the best European masters (who were probably Flemish and German, but working in the French style).

History of Budapest
The rest of the museum is a rather old-fashioned and less than inspiring exhibition concerning the history and development of Buda and Pest from the Neanderthal period to the Romans (second floor) and from the Romans to the Magyar conquest (first floor). For the subsequent history of Budapest, you should visit the excellent Kiscelli Museum in Óbuda (see p73).

MUSEUMS IN THE PALACE COMPLEX
WING A:
Ludwig Collection Open: Tue–Fri & Sun 10am–6pm, Sat 9am–5pm.
www.ludwigmuseum.hu
WINGS B, C, D:
Magyar Nemzeti Galéria (Hungarian National Gallery) Open: Tue–Sun, all year round 10am–6pm.
Admission charges (free on Sat).
www.mng.hu For English-speaking guide: *tel (06 1) 375 7533, ext 423.*
WING E:
Budapesti Történeti Múzeum
Open: Wed–Mon, Apr–Nov 10am–6pm; Dec–Mar 10am–4pm. Admission charge.
www.btm.hu For the topographical and 19th century part of the Budapest History Museum, see Kiscelli Múzeum (*p73*).
WING F:
Országos Széchényi Könyvtár
Reading room open: Mon 1–9pm, Tue–Fri 9am–9pm, Sat 9am–5pm. *www.oszk.hu* Reader's ticket required.
Szent György tér 2. Tel: (06 1) 224 3700.

The former Legújabbkori Történeti Múzeum (Museum of Contemporary History) – now closed – documented the history of the working class movement in Hungary and was highly ideological. Its valuable photographic archives now belong to the National Gallery.

Ludwig Múzeum (Ludwig Collection)

The building which housed the Museum of Contemporary History still contains a collection of modern art originally loaned, now donated, by the German industrialist Peter Ludwig. There are about 200 exhibits

divided into two permanent displays: 'Art from the 1950s to the Present' and 'Hungarian Art from the 1960s to the Present'.

Magyar Nemzeti Galéria (Hungarian National Gallery)

The National Gallery and its 70,000 pieces were moved to the reconstructed Royal Palace in 1975. Only Hungarian works (or those executed in Hungary) are displayed here (European masters and other antiquities may be found in the Museum of Fine Arts, *see pp78–9*).

Permanent Displays

• Medieval and Renaissance sculpture, including relics of the old Buda and Visegrád palaces – ground floor.
• Gothic wooden sculpture and panel painting from the 14th to the 15th century, mostly from Upper Hungary (now Slovakia) – ground floor.
• Late-Gothic triptychs, including a celebrated *Annunciation* (1506) by Master MS – first floor.
• Baroque art, dominated by Austrian artists who gained commissions in Hungary in the wake of the Counter-Reformation, some containing interesting Hungarian portraits – first floor.
• Hungarian painting and sculpture of the 19th century. Look out for the charming Biedermeier genre and landscape paintings by Miklós Barabás, and the scenes from Hungarian history

Donáth's *Turul Bird*, mythical begetter of the Hungarian royal line

works by Gyula Benczúr and Viktor Madarász) – first floor. In another wing first floor) are Hungarian Post-Impressionists and rooms devoted to the most successful Magyar painter ever, Mihály Munkácsy. His wide range includes the evocative *Dusty Road*, the melodramatic *Condemned Cell*, and the musing *Yawning Apprentice*.

Hungarian painting and sculpture of he 20th century. The highlights here are he dream-like work of Tivadar Csontváry Kosztka, the pointillism of ózsef Rippl-Rónai, and, especially, the utput of the *plein air* artists' colony at Nagybánya. Károly Ferenczy's *October* is erhaps the loveliest picture in the allery – second floor.

The Palatine's Crypt

very hour (usually) you can join a uided tour to see the marble-clad aulted crypt and sarcophagus of the opular Palatine, Archduke Joseph of Habsburg.

Monuments around the Royal Palace

n front of the palace's main entrance is ózsef Róna's equestrian statue of Prince ugene of Savoy, the hero of the Turkish vars, built in 1900. Emperor Franz oseph paid for its erection after the own that had commissioned it (Zenta) an out of money.

To the north is Gyula Donáth's *Turul Bird* (1903), the mythical begetter of the rpád line of kings. In the western ourtyard is Alajos Stróbl's *Matthias ountain*, a sculptural representation of ballad by Mihály Vörösmarty, which ells the story of 'beautiful Ilonka', who net and fell in love with King Matthias

Statue of Prince Eugene of Savoy, the Hammer of the Turks

when he was out hunting incognito. She pined away and died when she realised that her love was hopeless.

Next to the fountain is György Vastagh's lively sculpture showing a *puszta* cowboy breaking in a horse.

Országos Széchenyi Könyvtár (Széchenyi National Library)

The library was founded in 1802 by Count Ferenc Széchenyi, father of the great reform politician, István Széchenyi. By law it receives a copy of every Hungarian book or journal and also collects all scholarly works relating to Hungary.

Churches

Belvárosi Plébániatemplom (Inner City Parish Church)

The history of Pest is reflected in the many-layered architecture of the plébániatemplom. Succeeding a church built on the ruins of Roman Contra-Aquincum, a burial chapel for St Gellért was erected here in 1046. Parts of a subsequent 12th-century basilica survived Gothic reconstruction in the 15th century. The Turks turned the choir into a mosque, as a *mihrab* (prayer niche) in the south wall testifies. Baroque conversion under György Paur was begun in 1725 and two further alterations took place in the 19th century. Twentieth-century restorers have laid bare medieval details such as the sedilia in the sanctuary and the Italian-style 15th-century fresco of the crucifixion.

The modern panels of the altar, depicting the life of the Virgin Mary, are the work of Pál C Molnár. At the end of the side aisle are two beautiful Renaissance tabernacles in red marble,

Ornamentation in the Inner City Parish Church

probably made by craftsmen at the court of Matthias Corvinus. The statue of St Florian recalls fires that badly damaged Pest several times in the early 18th century. (*See also p32.*)
Március 15 tér 2. Tel: (06 1) 318 3108. Metro: to Ferenciek tere.

Egyetemi Templom (University Church)

It is thought that the Dominicans had a church on this site in the Middle Ages, later turned into a mosque by the Turks. The Hungarian order of Paulites acquired it in the 1720s. Their church was not completed until 1742 (the towers in 1770), and was probably designed by the Salzburg architect, Andreas Mayerhoffer.

The Inner City Parish Church

The Rococo ceiling frescoes of the *Adoration of the Virgin* (1776) are by the Bohemian Johann Bergl, while the beautifully carved pews are the work of Paulite monks. The adjacent theological library also contains finely carved shelves and galleries, but may be difficult of access. (*See also p31.*)
Egyetem tér 5–7/Papnövelde u. 7. Tel: (06 1) 318 0555. Metro: to Kálvin tér.

Evangélikus Templom (Lutheran Church)

Emperor Joseph II's Tolerance Patent (1781) allowed the building of Protestant churches (but without towers) in areas where a minimum of 100 Protestant families existed to form a parish. The Lutheran Church of Pest, designed by Mihály Pollack, was completed by 1809 and József Hild added the Neo-Classical portico in 1856. The adjacent Evangélikus Országos Múzeum (Lutheran Museum) is also worth a visit: its most treasured possession is Martin Luther's will, acquired in 1804. Around four per cent of Hungarians are Lutherans.
Deák Ferenc tér 4. Tel: (06 1) 317 4173. Museum open: Tue–Sun 10am–6pm in summer, up to 4pm in winter. Metro: to Deák Ferenc tér.

Ferenciek Temploma (Franciscan Church)

The Italianate Baroque church of the Franciscans in Pest was finished in 1758, but its fairy-tale tower was added in 1858. The 19th-century frescoes of the interior are by Károly Lotz. A marked pew shows where the composer Franz Liszt used to sit.

Ferenciek tere 9. Tel: (06 1) 317 3322. Metro: to Ferenciek tere.

Óbudai Plébániatemplom (Óbuda Parish Church)

Károly Bebó is responsible for much of the notable interior of the charming Baroque church of St Peter and St Paul in Óbuda. The carved pulpit is especially fine Rococo work, with depictions of the Good Shepherd, Mary Magdalene, and allegories of Faith, Hope, and Charity.
Lajos utca 168. Tel: (06 1) 368 6424. HÉV: to Árpád híd; or tram 1 to Szentlelek tér.

The historic Matthias Church is dealt with in the section on Castle Hill (*see p111*). Some of the churches described here and on pages 56–7 are also featured in the different Walks (*see p31, p32, & p35*).

Inside the Óbuda Parish Church

Református Templom
(Calvinist Church)

József Hofrichter's rigid Neo-Classical, somewhat provincial church of 1830 is not much enhanced by the portico added in 1838. The inside is more pleasing, with long galleries by József Hild and stained glass by Miksa Róth, the latter showing Protestant Hungarian heroes and Calvin himself. The treasury contains goldsmiths' work of the 17th to 19th centuries. (*See p31.*)
Kálvin tér 7. Tel: (06 1) 217 6769.
Metro: to Kálvin tér.

Szent Anna Templom
(St Anne's Church)

The original architect of the city's best loved Baroque church (1761) is unknown, but the design is clearly

St Anne's, one of the loveliest Baroque churches in the city

Italianate. Above the doorway are sculptures representing Faith, Hope, and Charity; further up are St Anne with Mary, the Buda coat of arms, and a golden eye of God with angels. Inside, note the Neo-Baroque ceiling frescoes by Pál C Molnár (1938) and the graceful pulpit by Károly Bebó.
Batthyány tér 7. Tel: (06 1) 201 3404.
Metro: to Batthyány tér.

Szent István Bazilika
(St Stephen's Basilica)

Budapest debtors say 'I'll settle up when the Basilica is finished', an allusion to the 54 years (1851–1905) it took to build the church. After the dome of the Neo-Classical original collapsed (January 1868), Miklós Ybl rebuilt the church to a Neo-Renaissance plan. Franz Joseph, attending the consecration, is said to have cast anxious eyes at the dome, whose previous fall, according to an eye-witness, made a 'horrible roar' and broke 300 windows in the neighbourhood. After Ybl's death, József Kauser completed the work. St Stephen's is not basilical in form, but was granted basilical status by Pope Pius XI on the occasion of the Eucharistic Congress held in Budapest in 1938.

Ybl's replacement dome is one of the most striking features of the interior, 22m in diameter and 96m high. Leading academic artists of the day contributed to the church's decoration. Károly Lotz designed the dome mosaics, while Gyula Benczúr painted the popular *St Stephen Dedicating his Country to the Virgin Mary* (south transept). The marble statue of St Stephen on the high altar is by Alajos Stróbl.

The façade of St Stephen's Basilica and . . .

The star attraction is the Szent Jobb, claimed to be the mummified right hand of St Stephen (at the end of the passage to the left of the altar). In 1938, it was paraded round Hungary in a gold-painted train, but nowadays its excursions are limited to a circuit of the church on St Stephen's Day (20 August). (*See* Walk *on p84.*)
Szent István tér 1. Tel: (06 1) 317 2859. Metro: to Deák Ferenc tér or Arany Fános utca.

Szerb Templom (Serbian Church)
The Serbian merchants and craftsmen of Pest had their own printing house and other institutions, including this attractive Baroque church (1698). The architect is thought to have been Andreas Mayerhoffer. The iconostasis dates from 1850. Paintings of scenes from the life of Jesus, the saints, and the apostles are by Károly Sterio. (*See p31.*)
Szerb utca 2–4. Metro: to Kálvin tér.

Szervitak Temploma (Servite Church)
The Servites, one of the religious orders invited to Hungary during the Counter-Reformation, hung on in Pest, although the City Council once forced them to move, and on another occasion compelled them to rebuild on their own plot in a manner the Council thought fitting to the metropolis. Their church is in a pleasantly harmonious Baroque style and contains some fine sculpture, notably János Thenny's statues of St Stephen, St Joachim, St Anne, and St Ladislas.
Szervita tér 6. Tel: (06 1) 318 5536. Metro: to Deák Ferenc tér.

. . . its magnificent dome

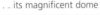

Gardens and Parks

Európapark

This pleasant grove lies close to Ostrom utca below Bécsi kapu (Vienna Gate) on Castle Hill. In 1972, 100 years after the unification of Buda, Óbuda, and Pest, the mayors from various cities round the world planted trees here, each of them a local symbol of growth and prosperity. There are 16 species, among them Turkish hazel and Japanese cherry.
Várbusz from Moszkva tér to Bécsi kapu tér.

Jubileumi Park, Gellért-hegy (Jubilee Park on Gellért Hill)

The Gellért Hill is criss-crossed with paths (*see pp42–3*) that afford fine views of Pest. On the southwestern side of the

Budapest's parks are full of colour

hill, below the Citadella and the Freedom Monument, the Jubilee Park was laid out in 1967 to mark the passage of 50 years since the Russian Revolution. The park is a delightful place for walking, with paths climbing from terrace to tree-lined terrace.
Gellért-hegy is reached by trams 18, 19, 47 & 49. Bus: 86 to Szent Gellért tér.

Margit Sziget (Margaret Island)

Margit Sziget is named after Béla IV's daughter, who retired to a convent here and is said to have lived a life of exemplary piety. The Turks went to the other extreme, finding the sanctuary a conveniently secure place to keep the Pasha's harem. Palatine Joseph acquired possession in 1796, built a villa here, and laid out a fine park with a rose garden. In 1869, it was opened to the public and became a favourite excursion area for Budapestians. The Habsburg governors sold it to the city in 1908. (*See pp44–5*.)
Bus: 26 from Nyugati pályaudvar.

Millenáris Park (Millennium Park)

The former industrial area of the Ganz fabrik was converted in 2001 to this lovely modern park and exhibition halls – an example of new city development.
Between Margit körút and Marczibányi tér (Buda side) behind the Mammut shopping mall. Metro: to Moszkva tér. Trams: 4 & 6 to Szena tér.

Népliget (People's Park)

This now somewhat decayed park, the biggest in the capital, was laid out in the 1860s and much embellished with

Buda

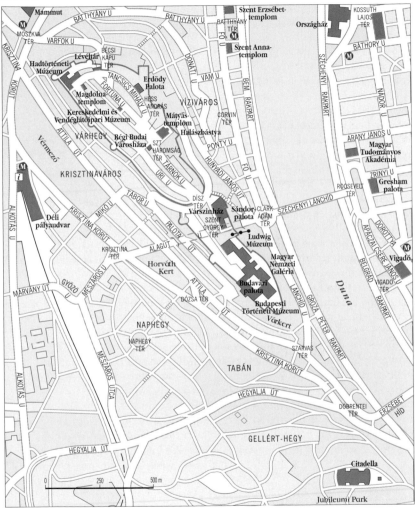

monuments and fountains at the time of the union of Buda and Pest. It includes the Planetarium and a laser theatre.
Metro: to Népliget.

Városliget (City Woodland Park)
See pp116–17.

Vérmező (Field of Blood)
The leader of the Jacobin conspiracy of 1795, Ignác Martinovics, was executed here, hence the name given to this grassy area west of Castle Hill. The meadow covers the site of a medieval village.
Bus: 5 from Március 15 tér.

Gül Baba Türbéje (Tomb of Gül Baba)

The only significant Turkish monument to survive in Budapest, other than baths, is the tomb of Gül Baba, situated in a sunken rose garden at the top of the cobbled Gül Baba utca on Rózsadomb.

Gül Baba was a dervish, a luminary of the Bektashi mendicant order whose members cultivated the arts and engaged in agriculture in time of peace, but were ready to die as martyrs (*ghazi*) in time of war. He died during a thanksgiving service for the conquest of Buda, held in the Matthias Church (hastily transformed into a mosque) on Friday, 2 September, 1541. The Sultan himself is said to have been among the pallbearers as this distinguished Islamic scholar was laid to rest. Hungarians later credited him with the introduction of rose cultivation in Hungary. Later still, he entered popular mythology as a harmless figure of fun (he crops up in this role in an operetta by Jenő Huszka based on a story by Mór Jókai). The tomb was built on the orders of the Pasha between 1543 and 1548. It is a modest octagonal building with a hemispherical copper dome topped by a crescent moon. Originally, this was a place of pilgrimage for pious Muslims and there was also a

Inside the Kerepesi Cemetery

tekke (monastery) next to it. The Jesuits turned it into a chapel in 1689 and kept it until their dissolution in 1773. The Turkish government acquired the shrine in 1885 and donated some of the furniture – the rest has been given by Hungarian Muslims.

Mecset utca 14. Tel: (06 1) 355 8849.
Open: May–Sep, Tue–Sun 10am–6pm;
Oct 10am–4pm. Admission charge.
Trams: 4, 6 to Márgit híd, then a short walk uphill or bus 191 from Nyugati pályaudvar metro to Apostol utca, then downhill.

Kerepesi Temető (Kerepesi Cemetery)

Beyond the Eastern Railway Station (Keleti pályaudvar) Pest begins to spread itself with sports stadia, race tracks, and the huge (90,000sq m) Kerepesi Cemetery. The cemetery, Hungary's

The simple tomb of the Dervish Gül Baba

national pantheon, is no longer in use. Its status as a patriotic shrine was scarcely enhanced by the inclusion of Communist worthies, buried with full honours traditionally supplied by the unsavoury 'Workers' Militia'. The last to be entombed in the 'Pantheon of the Working Class Movement' was János Kádár in 1989.

Perhaps it was the disagreeable company that prompted the son of László Rajk to have his father's remains removed from the area: Rajk Senior (who was just as unscrupulous as his tormentors, but spoke well) was executed after a show trial in 1949, Kádár himself having successfully extracted his 'confession' in prison. His rehabilitation and reburial in 1956 was attended by 250,000 and lit the fuse for the revolution of that year. Another notable absentee from Kerepesi is Imre Nagy, the ill-fated prime minister of 1956, who was reburied in the Pest Municipal Cemetery in 1989 after a ceremony in his honour on Heroes' Square. Previously, he had lain in an unmarked grave.

Some distance from the burial place of those who enslaved their fellow-countrymen is that of Lajos Kossuth, who led them temporarily to freedom in 1848. The tomb is a rhetorical monument crowned by a figure holding aloft the torch of Liberty. Other major public figures who have graves of honour here include Lajos Batthyány (prime minister of the independent government of 1848), and Ferenc Deák (architect of the Compromise with Austria, 1867). József Antall, the first post-Communist prime minister, was buried here, next to Kossuth, on 18 December, 1993. The world of the arts is represented by Ferenc Erkel, the actress Lujza Blaha, and Zsigmond Móricz (an early-20th century writer in the Zola mould). *Main entrance in Fiumei út.* *Tram: 24 from Keleti pályaudvar.*

Kerepesi Cemetery, last resting place of Hungarian heroes and villains

HŐSÖK TERE
Heroes' Square

The 2.6-km long boulevard of Andrássy út ends in the east at Heroes' Square, the site chosen at the end of the last century for the millennial memorial (*see map p66*). Every monument on the square relates to the theme of national identity along with the triumphs and catastrophes of Magyar history.

Millenniumi Emlékmű (Millenium Monument)

In the vast square that confronts you as you enter from the west, the dominant object is György Zala's 36-m high Millennium Monument. At the top of an elegant Corinthian column is a representation of the Archangel Gabriel, holding the Crown of St Stephen in one hand and the Apostolic Cross in the other. According to legend, the Archangel appeared to King Stephen in a dream and told him to convert the Hungarians to Christianity. The Apostolic or Patriarchal Cross (with two horizontal bars) signifies King Stephen's role as converter of the nation.

At the base of the column are Zala's romantic representations of the leaders of the seven Magyar tribes who entered the Carpathian

Basin in AD 896. The depiction of these fearsome-looking chieftains astride their horses represents the apotheosis of romantic historicism at the turn of the century. In front of the column and the seven chieftains is a simple memorial to the Hungarian soldiers who fell in two world wars, with a guard of honour on political anniverseries.

The Colonnade

Behind the Archangel Gabriel column is a crescent-shaped colonnade with statues of significant figures in Hungarian history placed above friezes showing crucial historical events. From left to right the statues represent: St Stephen, St Ladislas, Kálmán Könyves (Beauclerc), Andrew II, and Béla IV (all of the Árpád dynasty); the Angevin rulers Charles Robert and Louis the Great; János Hunyadi (Regent 1445–52) and Matthias Corvinus; then four Transylvanian princes (replacing Habsburgs); and finally, the 19th-century revolutionary leader Lajos Kossuth (*see p88*). Above are allegorical sculptures of War and Peace, Work and Wealth, Knowledge and Glory.

Statue of István Bocskai, part of the pantheon on Heroes' Square

Pest

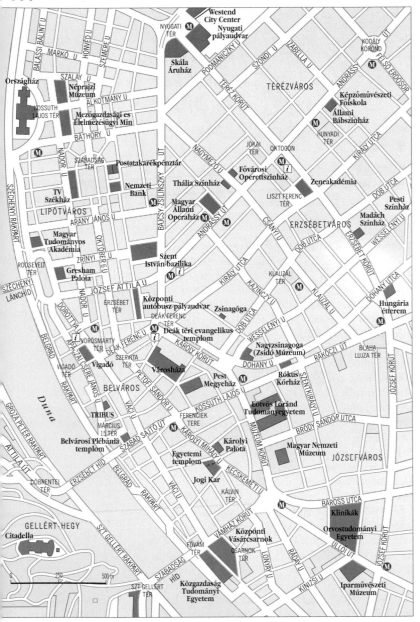

Relief of battling Hungarians on Heroes' Square

Symbolism and Politics on Heroes' Square

After the Ausgleich (Compromise) with Austria in 1867, a degree of sovereignty was at last restored to Hungary after centuries of absolute rule from Vienna. But the fact that the King-Emperor (Franz Joseph) was still a Habsburg posed delicate problems for those constructing a monument to national achievement which, on the one hand, had to make concessions to Magyar pride, and, on the other, had to avoid any offence to the ruling house.

Habsburg rule effectively began in 1526 following defeat by the Turks at the Battle of Mohács. In dealing with the period before this, national glory under native and foreign dynasties could be confidently asserted – sometimes providing a salutary historical reminder for the Habsburgs at the same time. An example is the frieze under the colonnade statue of Charles Robert of Anjou which depicts the battle of the Marchfeld (1278); it was here that Rudolf of Habsburg's victory over Ottakar of Bohemia was secured by the Hungarian king, Ladislas IV, and his Cumanian cavalry.

Originally, the colonnade contained the statues of five Habsburgs: Ferdinand I, Charles VI, Maria Theresa, Leopold II, and Franz Joseph himself. These were generally the

THE MILLENNIAL CELEBRATIONS

In 1881 the Budapest Council submitted a proposal to the National Assembly for a monument to mark the arrival of the Hungarians in the Carpathian Basin some 1,000 years earlier. Scholars were unable to agree on the exact date of their arrival. In the end, a millennium of 1896 was chosen. György Zala and Albert Schickedanz were given the task of preparing a monumental scheme to celebrate the millennium and 'inspire a sense of continuity and permanence'.

The statues and monuments were actually erected after the millennial celebrations (for which the first stretch of underground railway was also built). The 1896 exhibition celebrating Magyar achievements took up the whole area of the Városliget (*see* pp116–17) and was approached by a triumphal arch on Heroes' Square. It attracted over six million visitors.

ones least offensive to Hungarian sensitivities, or even, like Maria Theresa, held in some affection. Under the Communist Republic of Councils (1919), the Habsburg statues were removed and the Millennium Monument turned into a giant obelisk, the front of which featured Karl Marx being fawned upon by grateful workers. Under the Regent, Miklós Horthy, the Habsburgs were returned to their niches, but were once again removed by the Communists after World War II, to be replaced by the independent Transylvanian princes of the 17th and 18th centuries, István Bocskai, Gábor Bethlen, Imre Thököly, and Ferenc Rákóczi.

The Rákosi regime would have liked to sweep away the whole monument, since its symbolism was not appropriate to their historical script.

Műcsarnok (Hall of Art)

Schickedanz and Herzog were the architects for the building on the south side of Heroes' Square, the Hellenistic Műcsarnok (1895). It proved useful during World War I, when it was requisitioned as a military hospital. The mosaic on the pediment, *St Stephen as Patron of the Arts*, was a later addition. The gallery mostly shows work by modern Hungarian artists.

On the north side of Heroes' Square is the Museum of Fine Arts, devoted to non-Hungarian art (*see pp78–9*). This imposing piece of Hellenistic histori-cism (1906) was also designed by Zala's co-worker on the Millennium project, Albert Schickedanz, with Fülöp Herzog. *Dózsa György út 37.*

Hősök tere is reached from Vörösmarty tér by the metro (földalatti – yellow line).

The pantheon of great Hungarians in the Colonnade

Walk: Oktogon to Gundel Étterem

This walk is mostly concerned with the legacy of the Millennial celebrations of 1896, held 1,000 years after the Hungarians first entered the Carpathian Basin.
Allow 2 hours.

Start from the metro station (yellow line) at Oktogon and walk east along Andrássy út.

1 Former ÁVH Headquarters – Andrássy Út 60

The ÁVH, the secret police of the Communist regime, had their headquarters in this building, which they took over from their Nazi counterparts. A plaque on the wall recalls that Cardinal Mindszenty was tortured here. The policeman responsible recently died, uncharged, at a ripe old age. The building is now home to the new Terror Háza Múzeum (Museum of the House of Terror, *tel: (06 1) 374 2600, www.terrorhaza.hu*).

2 Kodály Körönd

The roundabout is named after the composer Zoltán Kodály, whose

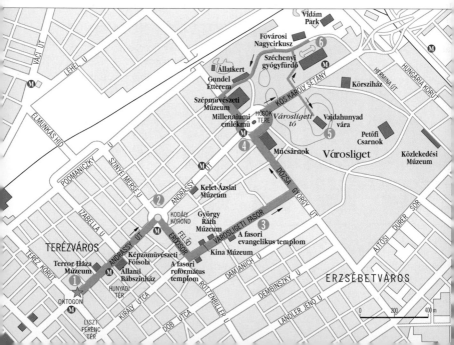

Memorial Museum is at No. 1. At each
corner of the roundabout are statues of
Hungarian heroes of the Turkish wars.
*Turn right down Felső erdősor utca and
left into Városligeti fasor.*

3 Városligeti Fasor

At Városligeti fasor 5–7 is Aladar Árkay's
curious Fasori református templom
(Calvinist Church, 1913), combining
Hungarian vernacular with Finnish
influence. Over the porch are tiles
decorated with Magyar folk motifs,
which recur in the impressive interior.
No less remarkable, at Városligeti fasor
17, is Samu Pecz's Neo-Gothic Fasori
evangelikus templom (Lutheran Church,
1905). Gyula Benczúr painted the
Adoration of the Magi on the high altar.
At No. 12 is the György Ráth Múzeum,
containing Chinese and Japanese
artefacts. All along the tree-lined avenue
are elegant early-20th century villas, one
of which belonged to the well-to-do
family of the Marxist philosopher,
György Lukács.
*You can rejoin Andrássy út via Bajza
utca, or walk down to Dózsa György út
and turn left, passing the area where the
Communists held their propaganda rallies.*

4 Hősök Tere (Heroes' Square)

The square (*see p62*) is a national focus
of identity created for the Millennial
celebrations. On your right is the
Műcsarnok, an exhibition hall devoted
to modern art; on your left is the
Szépművészeti Múzeum (Museum of
Fine Arts, *see pp78–9*).

  The column in the centre of the square
is topped by the figure of the Archangel
Gabriel who, according to one legend,

was responsible for suggesting to Pope
Sylvester that he send a crown to King
Stephen in AD 1000 (*see p8*). Round the
base are mounted Magyar chieftains.
Kings and national heroes are displayed
in the pantheon at the rear.
*Beyond Heroes' Square cross the
Városligeti tó (lake) on the Kós Károly
sétány and turn right down the
Vajdahunyad sétány. Rowboats are
available on the lake in summer, and in
winter it becomes an ice rink.*

5 Vajdahunyad Vára
(Castle of Vajdahunyad)

Ignác Alpár's architectural fantasy on
the artificial island (*see p117*) boasts a
replica of Vajdahunyad Castle in
Transylvania. Other features include a
replica of the Romanesque cathedral at
Ják (Western Hungary), the Agricultural
Museum, and the statue of King Béla
III's anonymous chronicler.

6 Széchenyi Gyógyfürdő/
Zoo/Gundel Étterem

A stroll back across the Városliget brings
you to the Széchenyi Baths (*see p37*), the
zoo (Állatkert), Vidám Park (amusement
park), and the celebrated Gundel
Étterem (restaurant) at Állatkerti út 2,
now restored to its early-20th century
splendour by George Lang.
*The metro (yellow line) leaves from
Hősök tere, or Szechenyi furdo.*

Zoltan Kodály Memorial Museum
Tel: (06 1) 342 8448. Open: Wed 10am–
4pm, Thu–Sat 10am–6pm, Sun 10am–2pm.
György Ráth Museum
Tel: (06 1) 342 3916. Open: Tue–Sun
10am–5.45pm (till 4pm in winter).

Hungarian National Style

'Hungarian form did not exist – but it will now!' With these auspicious words Ödön Lechner (1845–1914) began his idiosyncratic quest for a national style. His remark echoes and complements a similar declaration by Count István Széchenyi in 1830: 'Many people think "Hungary once was": I want to believe "she will be".'

The Institute for Geology

Lechner spent some years abroad, and English and French influences are present in his early work. When Jugendstil/Art Nouveau arrived in Hungary, he embraced it enthusiastically.

Detail from Ödön Lechner's fine Post Office Savings Bank

In a whimsical interpretation of ethnic roots he happily incorporated Indian, Persian, and Moorish motifs, together with ornamentation derived from Hungarian folk art.

Magisterially indifferent to mere technical details of weight or stress, which he left to his long-suffering partners (notably Gyula Pártos), Lechner was equally cavalier about expense – or so his enemies in the city council claimed (in the end they managed to prevent him getting any more commissions). For his part, Lechner pointed out that he used brick, which was cheaper than the stone used by his main rival, and majolica, which was easier to clean. When asked why he ornamented the backs of roofs, which could not be seen, he replied: 'Why shouldn't the birds have something to enjoy?'

LECHNER BUILDINGS
Iparművészeti Múzeum (Museum of Applied Arts)
The restored Moorish-style stucco of the interior is superb. The stairwell's tiers of undulating carved banisters are topped by an attractive stained-glass cupola. *Üllői út 33–37. Tel: (06 1) 465 5100. Open: 10am–6pm (until 4pm Dec–Mar).*

Closed: Mon. Metro: to Ferenc konit, or
rams 4 & 6 to Ulloi út.

Magyar Állami Földtani Intézet
Institute for Geology)

Pale yellow walls, strips of brown
brickwork, and a light blue ceramic roof
topped by a huge globe make this one of
Lechner's most eye-catching buildings.
Stefánia út 14. National Geological
Museum tel: (06 1) 267 1427.
Metro: to Népstadion, then trolley-bus 75.

Postatakarékpénztár
(Post Office Savings Bank)

The walls rise to crenellations of yellow
majolica; beyond these is a roof with
coloured hexagonal tiles, richly
ornamented with floral motifs, angel-
wings, dragons' tails, and other exotica.
The recurrent representations of bee
and honeycomb (originally also
reflected in the fittings of the interior)
symbolise the bank's activity (see p93).
Hold utca 4. Bus: 15 to Szabadság tér.

The Post Office Savings Bank building

Jugendstil Architecture

In Central Europe the German term 'Jugendstil' is applied to the Art Nouveau architecture that had its roots in the Paris of the 1890s. In Budapest, the word *szecesszió* – 'Secession style' – is also used, reflecting the influence of the famous Vienna Secession movement, established in 1897 in opposition to the conservative and academic elements that prevailed in the arts.

Gresham Palace – in need of a face-lift, but still a fine building

Jugendstil/Art Nouveau was a liberating force, sensual, richly ornamental, and prepared to draw eclectically on the world of nature and folklore for its motifs. Coming, as it did, with the upsurge of national consciousness in the countries of the Austro-Hungarian Empire, it is not surprising that idiosyncratic versions arose at local level.

Hungarian Jugendstil drew on current ideas about ethnic roots; in the works of Ödön Lechner this was carried further and developed into a so-called 'national style' (*see pp68–9*). However, all Jugendstil architects, whether leaning towards the approach of Lechner, or that of the Viennese Secession, or even that of the English Arts and Crafts movement, shared a common enthusiasm for exploiting materials such as ceramics, glass, and wrought-iron; a determination to avoid pattern-book repetition of forms was another characteristic principle. Though in public buildings individuality sometimes had to give way to official or commercial considerations, private villas for the wealthy (of which the vast majority were built at the beginning of the 20th century) provided an opportunity for architects to give free rein to their imagination and ingenuity.

Anyone interested in seeing some of these private houses should spend some time on either side of the outer reaches of Andrássy út. Examples of fine Jugendstil villas can be seen at Városligeti fasor 24 and 33, both designed by Emil Vidor; further out, at Ajtósi Dürer sor 25, is the villa built for the sculptor György Zala (co-organiser of the millennium memorial project), to a modified Lechner design.

Jugendstil Buildings

Although Ödön Lechner and his partner, Gyula Pártos (*see p68*) overshadow the rest, there were many interesting architects in early-20th century Budapest who built their own more or less idiosyncratic versions of Jugendstil. Their public and commercial buildings are all near the centre of Pest.

Gresham Palota (Gresham Palace)

This richly ornamented but crumbling block was built for the English insurance company of the same name by Zsigmond Quittner between 1905 and

1907. It has splendid stairways, stained glass by the Gödöllő artist, Miksa Róth, and a marvellous wrought-iron gate with peacock motifs. The palace is being converted to a Four Seasons luxury hotel. *Roosevelt tér 5. Buses: 16 & 105.*

Párizsi Udvar (Paris Arcade)

Henrik Schmahl's 1911 arcade has elaborate ornamentation on the façade as well as inside, where the coloured glass lights in the roof create an atmosphere of Alhambra-like mystery. *Ferenciek tere 5. Metro: Blue line to Ferenciek tere.*

Török Bankház (former Turkish Bank)

The glassed façade of the house (Henrik Böhm, Ármin Hegedűs, 1906) recalls French Art Nouveau. Miksa Róth made the striking mosaic in the gable, showing the Magyars offering allegiance to the Virgin Mary in her capacity as Patrona Hungariae.
Szervita tér 3. Metro: to Deák Ferenc tér.

On the same square, Béla Lajta's Rózavölgyi Ház (No. 5) betrays the influence of the controversial Viennese architect, Adolf Loos. There is another Jugendstil façade at No. 2.

Tomb of the Schmidl Family

It is worth the long trek to the Jewish Cemetery in Kőbánya to see the loveliest combined effort of Ödön Lechner and Béla Lajta, a gleaming gem of green and turquoise ceramic with gold edging, setting off delicate floral and star motifs. Inside is a stylised mosaic of the Tree of Life.
Izraelita temető, Kozma utca. Tram: 37 (long journey) from Népszínház utca.

The gable mosaic of the former Turkish Bank

Museums

Many of Budapest's more than 40 museums are in buildings of architectural interest, for example, the Ethnographical Museum (*see p78*). The most important are described here, while others are featured in the Walks. Museums in the complex of the Budavári palota (Royal Castle) are dealt with on pages 48–53. Many museums have free admission one day in the week – the day varies, so telephone first if you want to take advantage of this.

Moorish influence in the Museum of Applied Arts

Bartók Emlékház
(Béla Bartók Memorial House)

The composer Béla Bartók (1881–1945) lived in this villa from 1932 until his escape from Hungary in 1940. In the garden is a life-size statue of him by Imre Varga. Bartók's furniture has been reinstated in the rooms, together with some of his collection of Hungarian ceramics and textiles. The former living room, with its painted wooden ceiling, is used for concerts.
Csalán út 29. Tel: (06 1) 394 2100. Open: Tue–Sun 10am–5pm. Admission charge. Bus: 5 to Pasaréti tér, then 10 minutes' walk.

Anyone interested in Bartók's collaborator in the work of collecting Hungarian folk music can visit the Kodály Zoltán Emlékmúzeum (Zoltan Kodály Memorial Museum, *see pp66–7*).

Hardtörténeti Múzeum
(Museum of Military History)

Based in the former Palatine Barracks on Castle Hill, the display includes rooms devoted to the War of Independence (1848–9), World War I, and the 1956 revolution.
Toth Árpád sétany 40. Tel: (06 1) 356 9522. Open: Apr–Sep, Tue–Sun 10am–6pm (Oct–Mar until 4pm); www.extra.hu/opos/him.htm Admission charge. Várbusz from Moszkva tér to Bécsi kapu tér.

Iparművészeti Múzeum
(Museum of Applied Arts)

This Jugendstil museum was built by Ödön Lechner with Gyula Pártos in 1896 (*see p68*). The opening, attended by Franz Joseph himself, was part of the Millennial celebration of that year (*see p64*). Its oriental style of ornamentation reflected the architect's view that Magyars had originally come from the East.

A permanent exhibition showing design through the ages from the 12th century to present day opened in the mid-1990s.
Üllői út 33–7. Tel: (06 1) 217 5222. Open: Tue–Sun 10am–6pm (Dec–Mar until 4pm). Admission charge.

Metro: to Ferenc körút.
Trams: 4 & 6 to Üllői út.

Kiscelli Múzeum (Kiscelli Museum)

The most enjoyable of Budapest's
history museums chronicles the ages of
the city in displays combining nostalgia
with scholarship. A section on printing
shows the machine that printed Sándor
Petőfi's 'National Song', which roused
the populace in the 1848 revolution. It is
also worth lingering over the paintings,
mostly by 19th- and early-20th century
Hungarian masters.
Kiscelli utca 108. Tel: (06 1) 388 8560.
Open: summer, Tue–Sun 10am–6pm,
(4pm in winter). Admission charge.
Tram: 17; buses: 60 & 165 to Kiscelli utca.

Közlekedési Múzeum (Museum of Transport)

The origin of the collection lies in the
Millennial exhibition of 1896 (*see p64*).
Features include the history of the
Hungarian railway, historic vehicles, and
urban, water, and road transportation.
In the Petőfi Hall nearby is a permanent
display on the history of aviation. The
museum has an outlying branch: the
Földalatti Múzeum (Museum of the
Underground Railway) in the Deák
Ferenc tér metro station.
Városligeti körút 11. Tel: (06 1) 343 0565.
Open: Tue–Fri 10am–5pm, Sat & Sun
10am–6pm (Oct–Mar until 5pm).
Admission charge. Trolley buses: 72 & 74
to Hermina út.

Impressive statuary in the Kiscelli Museum

At the Liszt Museum, pause awhile, and imagine yourself in the company of the great composer

Liszt Ferenc Emlékmúzeum (Franz Liszt Memorial Museum)

The former apartment of Franz Liszt contains photographs and documents illustrating the composer's stormy life (1811–86). Liszt's books, musical scores, and much of his furniture have been preserved and there is a bronze of the great man's right hand by Alajos Stróbl.

Vörösmarty utca 35. Tel: (06 1) 322 9804. Open: Mon–Fri 10am–6pm, Sat 9am–5pm. Admission charge. Metro: to Vörösmarty utca.

Magyar Nemzeti Múzeum (Hungarian National Museum)

In 1802, the Széchenyi collection consisted of 11,884 docu-ments, 1,150 manuscripts, 142 volumes of maps and engravings, and 2,675 coins. It was

COUNT FERENC SZÉCHENYI (1754–1820)

The story of the Hungarian National Museum begins with Ferenc Széchenyi, father of 'the greatest Hungarian', István Széchenyi, and like him a patriot and moderniser.

Emperor Joseph II appointed him Viceroy of Croatia, but Széchenyi realised that Joseph's centralising and authoritarian approach left no room for national aspirations and resigned his post in 1786. He devoted himself to collecting artefacts and books with a view to donating them to the Hungarian nation; but even this gesture had to receive permission from Joseph's successor, Franz I, before it could be put into effect.

In his old age, Ferenc Széchenyi became fanatically conservative and seems to have suffered from religious melancholy, foreshadowing the mental instability that overtook his son in his final years.

valued at the then enormous sum of 160,000 forints and constituted the third most important national museum in Europe (after the Louvre and the British Museum). The museum enjoyed the support of the Palatine, Archduke Joseph, who became one of the trustees.

Expansion was at first hampered by application of an archaic law under which all objects discovered on Hungarian soil belonged to 'the state' and were transferred to Vienna. Then, in 1832, the great collection of the scholar Miklós Jankovich was acquired, marking the 'second founding' of the museum. At the same time the Palatine persuaded the Diet to allocate half a million forints (to come from the pockets of the nobility) for the construction of an edifice sufficiently splendid to be the repository of the nation's heritage.

The Collection

The leading Neo-Classical architect of the day, Mihály Pollack, was chosen to design the building, which was completed in 1837. Its façade recalls the Erechtheion on the Athens Acropolis, while the interior stairway sweeps up to a domed area reminiscent of the Pantheon in Rome.

The collection is divided into sections covering archaeology, the history of the Hungarian people, and the coronation insignia (crown, orb, chasuble, sceptre, and sword). Highlights include a room devoted to the 1848 revolution, the tent of a Turkish commander, and Renaissance stalls with beautiful marquetry from the church at Nyírbátor (northeast Hungary). The panelled Széchenyi Memorial Room contains a portrait of the founder by the Viennese

Statue of the poet János Arany in front of the National Museum

The Hungarian National Museum is counted among the most important museums in Europe

artist, Joseph Ender; round the top of the walls are the coats of arms of all the Hungarian counties.

The moth-eaten natural history collection on the top floor is in the process of being modernised.
Múzeum körút 14–16. Tel: (06 1) 338 2122; http://origo.hnm.hu Open: Tue– Sun 10am–6pm. Admission charge. Metro: to Kálvin tér; or trams 47, 49; buses 9 & 15.

Magyar Kereskedelmi és Vendéglátóipari Múzeum (Museum of Commerce and Catering)

The emphasis here is on everything to do with the catering and retail grocery trade. The recreated interiors of 19th-century food shops have great charm, and attractive period posters are on sale.
Fortuna utca 4. Tel: (06 1) 375 6249. Open: Wed–Fri

ST STEPHEN'S CROWN

A whole room is devoted to the royal insignia and the historic 'Holy Crown' (which actually post-dates the reign of St Stephen). It was returned to Hungary in 1978 from America, where it had been held in safekeeping since the end of World War II.

The crown is that of a Byzantine empress (*corona graeca*) to which an upper part (*corona latina*) was added, perhaps under Béla III (1172–96). The famous leaning cross on the top replaced an earlier one, a reliquary probably containing a fragment of the True Cross.

The *corona graeca* features portraits of the Byzantine Emperor Michael Ducas, flanked by his son and the Hungarian King Géza I (1074–7). The precious stones symbolise the four elements – sapphire for air, almandine (a kind of garnet) for fire, green glass for earth, and the rim of pearls for water.

10am–5pm, Sat & Sun 10am–6pm.
Admission charge. Várbusz: from
Moszkva tér to Szentháromság tér.

Magyar Mezőgazdasági Múzeum (Agricultural Museum)

This educational museum is another legacy of the millennial show. Of the 18 permanent displays, those on wine production, animal husbandry, and fishing are perhaps the most interesting. Horse breeding, also featured, is another field where Count István Széchenyi was active, importing English horses and methods to Hungarian studs and instituting the first horse races.
The museum is housed in the Baroque part of the Vajdahunyad Castle on Széchenyi-sziget, Olof Palme sétany, Városliget. Tel: (06 1) 343 3198.

Open: Tue–Sat 10am–4pm, Sun
10am–5pm (until 6pm in summer).
Admission charge. Metro: to Hősök tere.

MTA Zenetörténeti Múzeum (Museum of the History of Music)

Housed in the Baroque Erdődy Palace on Castle Hill, the collection has over 1,500 instruments, photographs, and musical documents. On the ground floor the permanent display deals with the manufacture of musical instruments, 18th- and 19th-century musical life, and Hungarian folk music. On the first floor is an archive of Bartók's manuscripts.
Táncsics Mihály utca 7. Tel: (06 1) 214 6770. Open: Mar–Oct, Tue–Sun 10am–5pm. Closed: Nov–Feb. Admission charge. Várbusz: from Moszkva tér to Bécsi kapu tér.

Everything to do with the art in the Museum of Commerce and Catering

Window in the Ethnographical Museum

Néprajzi Múzeum (Ethnographical Museum)

This museum is worth visiting to view the Neo-Renaissance interior of Alajos Hauszmann's building (1896). It began life as Hungary's Supreme Court, hence Károly Lotz's emblematic fresco on the ceiling of Justitia enthroned among the clouds, flanked by allegories of Justice, Peace, Sin, and Revenge.

The first floor is devoted to the traditional culture of the peoples of Hungary and was opened only in 1991. On the second floor, with the help of material from the museum's marvellous photographic archive, primitive cultures are documented, including that of the Ob-Ugrian Hanti and Manszi tribes in the Urals, ancestors of the Hungarians. *Kossuth Lajos tér 12. Tel: (06 1) 332 6340. Open: Tue–Sun 10am–6pm (4pm Nov– Feb). Admission charge. Metro: to Kossuth Lajos tér; or trams 2, 2A to Szalay utca.*

Semmelweis Orvostörténeti Múzeum (Semmelweis Museum of Medicine)

Named after Ignác Semmelweis (1818–65), the 'Saviour of Mothers' (*see p42*), whose father had a grocery shop here, the museum has a fascinating display of the history of medicine. There is also a complete Neo-Classical pharmacy designed by Mihály Pollack. *Apród utca 1/3. Tel: (06 1) 375 3533. Open: Tue–Sun 10.30am–5.30pm. Admission charge. Buses: 86, 5 & 78 to Szarvas tér. Tram: 19.*

Szépművészeti Múzeum (Museum of Fine Arts)

This is one of Europe's most substantial

rt collections, with 2,500 paintings on display, many derived from the Esterházy Collection purchased by the Hungarian state in 1870. The Italian school is particularly well represented with no less than five striking El Grecos.
Dózsa György út 41. Tel: (06 1) 343 9759. Open: Tue–Sun 10am–5.30pm (until 4pm Jan–Mar). Admission charge.
Metro to Hősök tere.

The façade of the Museum of Fine Arts

Music Venues

Új Színház (New Theatre – formally Parisiana)

This gem of theatre architecture was built as a cabaret by Béla Lajta in 1909. Alterations in the 1920s transformed Lajta's original Jugendstil into something closer to Art Deco. Its complete renovation won it the 1998 Europe Nostra Prize and has resulted in a glittering array of gilding, glasswork, and coloured marble.
Paulay Ede utca 35.
Tel: (06 1) 269 6021.
Metro: yellow line
(földallati) to Opera.

Erkel Színház (Erkel Theatre)

Renovation has left little of the building's original Jugendstil ornamentation intact, but its modern styling is itself attractive. In particular, the first-floor buffet area boasts two spectacular wall paintings by the Hungarian painter, Aurél Bernáth. At one end is *A Midsummer Night's Dream* and, at the other, a representation of Imre Madách's Faustian drama *The Tragedy of Man* (1861). Bernáth worked on the paintings between 1972 and 1973.

The National Opera, one of the most graceful work of Miklós Ybl

FERENC ERKEL (1810–93)

First director of the National Theatre, Erkel composed the quint-essential Hungarian opera *Bánk Bán* (1861), a musical setting of József Katona's patriotic play about a murder at the medieval Hungarian court. Erkel's music combined elements of the 18th-century *verbunkos* (played on recruiting drives), folk themes, and pre-Verdian opera. He also wrote the remarkably moving Hungarian national anthem (1844).

The New Theatre is a dazzling example of Art Deco

Köztársaság tér 30. Tel: (06 1) 333 0540.
Metro: (red line) to Blaha Lujza tér.

Magyar Állami Operaház (Hungarian State Opera)

In the 1870s it was decided to build an opera house in Pest of comparable grandeur to those in other European cities. Miklós Ybl won the commission and the opera house went up between 1875 and 1884. Built in a graceful Neo-Renaissance style, the technically sophisticated building embodies national pride combined with allusions to musical history. In niches either side of the main entrance are statues of Hungary's two greatest 19th-century composers: Ferenc Erkel (left) and Ferenc (Franz) Liszt (right). Four Muses are represented at the corners of the first storey, while famous composers line the balustrade above. The interior was decorated by Bertalán Székely, Mór Than, and Károly Lotz (note Lotz's

cupola fresco of Apollo on Olympus). Technical innovations included new fire precautions, several European theatres having recently burned down with loss of life. It was also something of a feat to install the auditorium's bronze chandelier weighing all of three tonnes. The cost ran to one million forints, most of it personally contributed by Emperor Franz Joseph.

Famous directors of the opera include Gustav Mahler (1888–91), Arthur Nikisch (1893–95), and Otto Klemperer (1947–50). In the 1930s (surprisingly, in view of the right-wing political climate), a number of modern operas were staged, including works by Stravinsky. *Andrássy út 22. Tel: (06 1) 353 0170; www.opera.hu Daily one-hour guided tours at 3pm & 4pm; English speaking guides available. Tours start from the entrance behind the Sphinx. For information, tel: (06 1) 332 8197. Metro: földallati (yellow line) to Opera, or bus 4.*

The Hungarian State Opera House

Fresco in the Music Academy

Pesti Vigadó (The Pest Concert Hall)

Mihály Pollack's original 'redoute' (ballroom) on this site fell victim to Austrian cannon fire from the Buda Hill during the 1848–9 War of Independence. Between 1858 and 1865, Frigyes Feszl built a new concert hall in a romantic style that incorporates oriental elements, reflecting the Asiatic roots of the Magyars: one of the figures in the frieze along the top of the façade is Attila the Hun, though the descent of the Hungarians from the Huns is more than doubtful. Further emphasis is placed on Magyar identity by the interior frescoes, scenes from Hungarian folk tales painted by Károly Lotz and Mór Than. 'Vigadó' is coined from *vigad* (to make merry – or have a ball), and the place has never lost its ballroom function (balls are still held here during the Shrovetide Carnival). Károly Alexy's dancing figures on the façade are thus absolutely appropriate.

Vigadó tér 1–2. Tel: (06 1) 318 4169/266 6177. Tram: 2 along the Pest embankment to Vigadó tér.

Zeneakadémia (Music Academy)

The first music academy was founded in 1875 by Franz Liszt and occupied three rooms above his flat in Irányi utca (Pest); there were then 38 students of piano and composition. After four years, demand was such that expansion became necessary, and the academy moved to Andrássy út (then Sugár út), where it occupied several floors and had its first auditorium. At the turn of the century the city decided to buy land for a much bigger music conservatory, subsequently built between 1904 and 1907 to plans by Flóris Korb and Kálmán Giergl.

The Liszt Ferenc Zenemüvészeti Főiskola (Franz Liszt High School for Music), to give it its official title, is a remark-able example of Korb and Giergl's idiosyncratic style, sometimes called 'Baroque Jugendstil'. Liszt is honoured with a huge statue (by Alajos Stróbl) over the main entrance and there are reliefs of two other founding professors, Ferenc Erkel and Róbert Volkmann. The building's exterior is pompous and heavy, but the interior is

MIKLÓS YBL (1814–91)

The Hungarian State Opera is probably the finest work of this great Hungarian architect, one of the best practitioners of so-called Historicism.

He built many hand-some apartment blocks in Pest, constructed around an internal courtyard, and offered spacious, high-ceilinged flats for the well-to-do. His public works reflect the grandeur and elegance of the Italian Renaissance. They include the second phase of St Stephen's Basilica and the huge Customs House (now the University of Economics). A statue of Ybl stands on the Danube bank below the castle, opposite his Várbazár complex (see p42).

striking, particularly in the iridescent colours of the Zsolnay ceramic fittings. In the first floor lobby is Aladár Körösfői-Kriesch's weird fresco *The Fountain of Youth*, with the sententious inscription: 'Those who search for life make a pilgrimage to the wellspring of art'. Its painter was a member of the artists' colony based in the village of Gödöllő, north of Budapest, whose members drew inspiration from Hungarian folk motifs and the English Pre-Raphaelites. Above the entrances to the auditorium on the ground floor Körösfői-Kriesch has painted two further frescoes representing sacred and profane music.

The large auditorium of the Music Academy seats 1,200 and is famous for its excellent acoustics. On the walls are images (painted by István Gróh and Ede Telcs) suggesting musical movements –

allegro, andante, adagio, and s*cherzo*. The smaller auditorium is used for chamber music and seats 400. The foyer has frescoes by János Zichy illustrating Hungarian musical history.

The Academy has had a distinguished past: many world famous performers such as Antal Doráti, George Szell, and Sir Georg Solti are numbered among its pupils. Its professors included all the great Hungarian composers: Ferenc Erkel, Béla Bartók, Zoltán Kodály, Leó Weiner and, of course, Liszt himself. The musical tradition here is unbroken, except for a bizarre interlude at the end of World War II when the building was used for the trial of Ferenc Szálasi, the Hungarian Fascist leader and psychopath.

Liszt Ferenc tér 8. Tel: (06 1) 341 4788. Trams: 4 & 6 to Király utca.

The Vigadó (Concert Hall)

Walk: Andrássy út

This walk takes you along the grandest boulevard of Pest, with a diversion through theatreland.
Allow 1½ hours.

Walk from the metro stop at Deák Ferenc tér across the east side of Erzsébet tér to the corner of Bajcsy-Zsilinszky út and József Attila utca.

1 International Trade Centre

Fans of Post-Modern architecture will appreciate the reflecting glass and futuristic sculpture of this building (Bajcsy-Zsilinszky út 12) by József Finta and associates. Finta's work is everywhere – he landed many of the plum contracts for hotels in the Communist period, including the Mariott and the Taverna.
A short detour down Bajcsy-Zsilinszky út brings you to St Stephen's Basilica (see pp46–7). Otherwise, bear diagonally to the right.

The State Opera House is a reflection of the country's grand tradition of music

2 Andrássy Út

Originally called Sugár (Radial) út, the boulevard has reflected political events in its many name changes. It was named Andrássy in 1885 after the distinguished prime minister and foreign minister (1823–90). Under Communism it was first called Stalin Avenue, then briefly Avenue of Hungarian Youth (during the 1956 revolution), then Avenue of the People's Republic, and now, once again, Andrássy út.

3 Magyar Állami Operaház (Hungarian State Opera)

This is one of Miklós Ybl's most opulent public buildings (*see p81*). Emperor Franz Joseph financed it and attended the opening on 27 September, 1884, when Ferenc Erkel's national opera *Bánk Bán* was performed.
Opposite the opera is an early building by Ödön Lechner (see pp68–9), now used by the corps de ballet. Go down the street beside it (Dalszínház utca) to Új Színház.

4 Új Színház (New Theatre)

The beautifully restored Art Deco theatre at Paulay Ede utca 35 is worth a visit simply to marvel at the interior (new, but recreated entirely in the spirit of the original).

5 Nagymező Utca

Further east on Andrássy út you come to Nagymező utca, once the Broadway of Budapest, and still boasting several theatres. Turn right down it; at No. 8 is the revived Ernst Múzeum, containing modern Hungarian and foreign art. The Jugendstil house (*tel: (06 1) 341 4355; open: Tue–Sun 10am–6pm*) was partly designed by Ödön Lechner, and the stained-glass window of the staircase is by József Rippl-Rónai.

Continue down Nagymező utca to the junction with Király utca, where you will see the late Baroque Terézváros Parish Church (1809). The open gangway running round the tower was the fire-watch. Inside are two fine Neo-Classical altars designed by Mihály Pollack (who built the National Museum). Across the junction at Király utca 47 is the extravagantly romantic Pékary-ház (National Savings Bank).

Note the statues of fierce Magyar chieftains over the portals.
Turn left along Király utca until you reach the southern end of Liszt Ferenc tér.

6 Zeneakadémia (Music Academy)

The Music Academy (1907) at Liszt Ferenc tér 8 (*see pp82–3*) is a bizarre mixture of Hungarian national style and eclectic features. Most striking is the gilded and ceramic-clad foyer. Symphonic, chamber, and choral works are performed in the auditorium, which is famous for its good acoustics.
Walk north through the square, passing the controversial modern statue of Franz Liszt (László Marton, 1986) and (at the Andrássy end) a statue of the poet Endre Ady, scourge of corrupt Magyar society, at the close of the 19th century. There is a tourist information bureau at the Liszt Ferenc tér 9–11. Turn right on Andrássy út for the metro at Oktogon.

Operetta was very popular during the period of the Austro-Hungarian Empire (1867–1918). Its origins were various: Austrian composers were inspired by the smash hits of Jacques Offenbach in Paris and by the tradition of the Wiener Volksstück (Viennese Popular Theatre). The Hungarian equivalent of the latter was the 'Népszínmű'. A musical rendering of Sándor Petőfi's poem about the life and love of a peasant boy from the Great Plain (*János Vitéz*) is a classic example of it. The characteristic figures represented in Hungarian 'Népszínmű' became the romantic clichés associated with a world that was already passing: the *csikós* (cowboy from the Great Plain), the *betyár* (a sort of Robin Hood), the *husar* (hussar), the *táblabíró* (provincial judges with feudal attitudes), together with a cast of peasants, 'heyducks' (personal gendarmerie of the magnates), and sentimentally portrayed gypsies.

The classic operetta is Johann Strauss's *Die Fledermaus* (1874), a witty and melodious satire on the decadent world of late 19th-century Vienna. The more strait-laced public in Budapest were initially slow to accept this, but then came the *Gypsy Baron* (1885), a work that symbolically united the two halves of the Empire. The libretto was based on a story by the greatest Hungarian novelist, Mór Jókai, and Johann Strauss wrote the music. It was an instant success.

The final period of operetta, which was increasingly a vehicle of escape from the realities of imperial decline and war, was dominated by Hungarian composers. Franz Lehár wrote two works that conquered the world – *The Merry Widow* (1905) and *Land of Smiles*

(1929). The prolific Emmerich Kálmán had an enormous success with the *Csárdás Princess* (1915). The frenetic energy and brittle glamour of its dance routines, set in the nightclub milieu, seem in retrospect to be the dance of death of the Empire itself:

'Every pulse is racing faster
While we dance and flirt and play:
The world outside is all disaster;
What care we till break of day . . .?'

Concert performance in the Vigadó – a popular venue for operatta

Ország ház

Parliament

The Parliamentary Tradition

Feudalism endured in Hungary right up to the 19th century, in some respects even into the 20th. The first glimmerings of modern parliamentarianism are contained in a memorandum submitted to the 1790–91 session of the Diet by a legal historian, József Hajnóczy.

Leading politicians of the Reform Era (István Széchenyi, Ferenc Deák, József Eötvös) advocated a widening and loosening of noble privilege, and the revolutionary government of 1848 actually raised the proportion of the population enjoying political rights from 2.5 per cent to 8 per cent.

The franchise was effectively narrowed again through tax qualifications in the 1870s and it was not until 1918 that universal suffrage briefly arrived. The Horthy period (partially) and that of Communism (totally) eclipsed democracy although, in between, free elections were held in 1947. The present government is the fourth to be democratically elected after the 43 years of totalitarianism.

The Building of the Parliament

A competition to design the proposed Parliament building was held in 1883. Only 19 plans were submitted (in contrast to the Berlin Reichstag, which attracted 180 entries); the small number may have been due to the specifications. Imre Steindl (1839–1902) won with a Neo-Gothic design, attacked by some as a 'German style', alien to the Hungarians; its supporters pointed out that Magyar and German culture had interacted fruitfully for centuries. In its style, river position, and cruciform layout the building showed the influence of Barry and Pugin's new Palace of Westminster on the Thames in London.

The exterior presents a dazzling array of finials, buttresses, towers, and a mighty dome. The gilded, marble-clad interior lives up to its role as a national

LAJOS KOSSUTH (1802–94)

A provincial lawyer and journalist, Kossuth made his first major political move by founding *Pesti Hírlap*, which (illegally) reported the proceedings of the Diet. He was briefly president of Hungary in 1848, but was forced into exile by the failure of the revolution. The rest of his life was spent abroad – in England, America, and Italy, where he died. He remains a potent symbol of the Hungarian struggle for freedom.

'If I were the ruler of Hungary, I would order all ships passing by on the Danube to stop for two minutes in front of the Houses of Parliament, so that travellers on board can admire, enjoy and learn from the beauty of the best Hungarian building.'

JÓZSEF KESZLER, writing in *Magyar Nemzet* when the Parliament was completed in 1902.

shrine. In the Speaker's Hall is Mihály Munkácsy's vast historical picture showing the Hungarians under Árpád receiving the homage of the Slav tribes of the Carpathian Basin.

Statuary around the Parliament

To the south is a statue of the 20th-century poet Attila József, seated overlooking the Danube he celebrated in verse. To the north is Mihály Károlyi, briefly prime minister of a democratic Hungary in 1918. On the square is the 18th-century freedom fighter, Ferenc Rákóczi II; and Lajos Kossuth to the north.

Kossuth Lajos tér. www.parliament.hu
Visits with English speaking guides offered
daily 10am & 2pm unless there is a session or ceremonial event. Tours start at Gate X just right of the main stairs. The guards will let you in to buy tickets just before the tour (tel: (06 1) 441 4904). Metro, trams 2 & 2A; trolleybuses 70 & 78; or Citybusz to Kossuth Lajos tér.

The Parliament in Statistics

One thousand workers took 17 years to build the Parliament. It is 265m long, 123m wide, and 96m high (the dome). It required 40 million bricks and 30,000 cubic metres of stone cladding, has 691 rooms, 17 gates, 29 staircases, and 12 elevators. Only 23 years after completion, renovation had to begin, as the stone chosen by Steindl was too soft.

Statue of Ferenc Rákóczi II, with Parliament beyond

PÁLYAUDVAROK (RAILWAY STATIONS)
Keleti Pályaudvar (Eastern Railway Station)

The second half of the 19th century saw the building of several iron and glass constructions in Budapest, chiefly market halls and railway stations, inspired by English and French models. Budapest's Eastern Railway Station (designed by Gyula Rochlitz and János Feketeházi, 1884) has a 44-m steel framework behind a rather grandiose Neo-Renaissance façade. Two British engineers are honoured with statues high up on the triumphal arch that spans the main entrance: on the right is James Watt (1736–1819), inventor of the steam engine; on the left, George Stephenson (1781–1848), builder of the famous *Rocket* locomotive in 1829.

In the departure hall on the left are sententious murals by Károly Lotz and Mór Thán (badly in need of restoration). Despite the station's name, many trains from the west arrive here, just as trains for the north and east leave from the Western Railway Station. The square in front of Keleti pályaudvar is named after Gábor Baross (1848–92), who was transport minister in the 1880s. He rationalised the Hungarian railway system by nationalising the six existing private railway companies.
Metro: to Keleti pályaudvar.

Nyugati Pályaudvar (Western Railway Station)

The first train on the first stretch of railway built in Hungary left for Vác on 15 July 1846 from the wooden predecessor to the present Western Railway Station. The architect responsible for this gracious example of industrial architecture (1877) was a Frenchman, August de Serres, and it was built by the famous Eiffel Company of Paris. In order to ensure that train services were not disrupted during construction work, the new station was built above and around the old one, which was demolished only when the work was complete.

The station has recently been restored, not quite authentically, since the (nonetheless attractive) blue paint on the ironwork is a Post-Modernist conceit. The former Royal Waiting Room, built for the arrival of Franz-Joseph and Elizabeth when they attended the millennial celebrations of 1896, is in the east wing. Its ceiling features the coats of arms of the Hungarian counties served by trains from this station. To the right of the main entrance a sumptuous restaurant, redolent of the bourgeois comforts of the railway age, still stands . . . now the most elegant McDonald's in Europe.
Teréz körút 109–111.
Metro: to Nyugati pályaudvar.

Roosevelt Tér (Roosevelt Square)

The best surviving architectural feature of the square, which was once ringed by fine Neo-Classical buildings, is the Magyar Tudományos Akadémia (Academy of Sciences) at the northern end. After István Széchenyi offered a year's income from his estates for the founding of such an academy, the rest of the money for it was raised from public subscription. A plaque on the east wall (Akadémia utca) shows Széchenyi making his offer. When he was asked how he would live in the meantime, he explained dryly: 'My friends are going to support me.' The Neo-Renaissance building was designed by a Berlin architect, Friedrich Stüler, and completed in 1861.

Széchenyi's statue stands before it; on the plinth are figures of classical deities symbolising his multifarious achievements – Minerva, Neptune, Vulcan, and Ceres.

Also on the square are statues of Ferenc Deák

(*see pp96–7*) and József Eötvös (1813–71), who reformed education in Hungary. The Jugendstil Gresham Palace (*see pp70–71*) stands next to the horrible 'Spinach Palace' (1979), while to the south is the no less horrible Inter-Continental (formerly Forum) Hotel, undoubtedly one of the worst architectural excrescences of the 1980s. Next to it is the less offensive Hyatt Regency (1982).

Bus: 16 to Roosevelt tér. Tram: 2 to Roosevelt tér or Eotvos tér.

The Eastern Railway Station

Walk: Deák Ferenc tér to Kossuth Lajos tér

The walk explores the institutional quarter of Pest.
Allow 2 hours.

Begin at Deák Ferenc tér and walk northwest across Erzsébet tér, leaving the international bus station on your right. On your left you will see the new Corvinus Kempinski Hotel, and on the corner of Harmincad utca, the huge former bank occupied by the British Embassy.

1 Danubius Kút (Danubius Fountain)

In the middle of Erzsébet tér is this triple-basined fountain, a copy of Miklós Ybl's beautiful original. The ladies perched on the lower bowl represent Danube tributaries – the Tisza, Dráva, and Száva.
Go through the passageway between the buildings on Bécsi utca to the south.

2 József Nádor Emlékmű

Johann Halbig's statue of Palatine Joseph of Hungary stands in the square. The sixth son of Emperor Leopold II, the Archduke was Palatine of Hungary from 1796 until his death 50 years later. He did much to realise Hungarian aspirations and moderate the policies of the Habsburg court in Vienna.
Turn left down József Attila utca and right into Roosevelt tér.

3 Roosevelt Tér

The square (*see pp90–91*) is flanked by the Inter-Continental and Hyatt Regency hotels at the southern end, and the elegant Magyar Tudományos Akadémia (Academy of Sciences) to the north. There are statues of 19th-century statesmen – József Eötvös (who reformed public education), Ferenc Deák (who organised the 1867

Compromise with the Habsburgs), and István Széchenyi (*see p100*). On the east side are the Ministry of the Interior, the Jugendstil Gresham Palota (Palace), now a Four Seasons luxury hotel, and an office block known as the 'Spinach Palace', because of its colour.

Walk along Akadémia utca and turn right down Széchenyi utca, which leads to Szabadság tér.

4 Szabadság Tér

The former stock exchange on the west side is now the TV Székház (Hungarian Television Centre); opposite is Ignác Alpár's eclectic Nemzeti Bank (National Bank – 1905). North of that is the Jugendstil American Embassy, where Cardinal Mindszenty took refuge during the 1956 revolution – and remained for 19 years. The statue nearby is of an American general who prevented Romanian troops from looting the National Museum in 1919. Ödön Lechner's marvellous Postatakarék-pénztar (Post Office Savings Bank, *see p69*) is round the corner (Hold utca 4). Just to the north is the Batthyány-örökmécses (Eternal Flame) commemorating the 13 Hungarian generals executed by the Habsburgs in 1849. The prime minister of the independent government,

Count Lajos Batthyány, was shot on this spot.

Walk on to Hold utca and turn left into Alkotmány utca, which leads to Kossuth Lajos tér.

5 Kossuth Lajos Tér

This vast space is dominated by Imre Steindl's Országház (Parliament, *see pp88–9*), the most ambitious construction project ever undertaken in Hungary. From 1885, some 1,000 labourers and craftsmen worked on it for 17 years. The vast red star of the Communist era was removed from the spire after 1989 at considerable cost. Alajos Hauszmann's Supreme Court (Kossuth Lajos tér 12), now the Neprajzi Múzeum (Ethnographical Museum), and the Mezögazdasági es Elelmézesügyi Min (Ministry of Agriculture) occupy the southeast side. The heroic statues on the square represent Lajos Kossuth and Ferenc Rákóczi II, 19th- and 18th-century heroes, respectively, of the struggle for independence.

Walk up past the 'White House', formerly the sinister headquarters of the Communists, now offices for Parliamentarians. Tram and bus stops are at the Pest end of Margit híd.

The Eternal Flame

Roman Remains

In the first century AD the Romans planted a garrison in the Pannonian Celtic settlement of Ak-Ink ('Abundant Waters') and Latinised the name to Aquincum. An outpost across the Danube was known as Contra Aquincum (*see p32*). The military camp, on what is now Flórián tér (Óbuda), had its own baths and a huge amphitheatre with seating for 15,000. The civilian town was 2km to the north and there were other strategic *castra* and watchtowers, components of the famous defensive system along the Danube known as the *limes*.

Roman column

Roman Remains in Óbuda
Tel: (06 1) 250 1650. Those that are accessible charge admission.
The **Amfiteátrum** (Military Amphitheatre), junction of Nagyszombat and Pacsirtamező utca (only exterior view), can be reached by buses 6 & 86 to Pacsirtamező utca.
Aquincum Museum, Szentendrei út 139. *Tel: (06 1) 250 1650.* Open May–Sep, Tue–Sun 10am–6pm; (until 5pm in Oct; closed Nov–Apr). HÉV to Aquincum, or buses 34, 42, 106 from Szentlélek tér, 106 from Árpad híd metro (Pest side).
The **Cella Trichora** (view from exterior only), at the junction of Hunor and Raktár utca. Buses 6, 84, 86; tram 1 to Flórián tér.
Herkules Villa, Meggyfa utca 19–21. *Tel: (06 1) 250 1650.* Open May–Oct by appointment only. Buses 6, 86 & 118 to Bogdáni út.
Military Baths Museum, Flórián tér 3–5. *Tel: (06 1) 250 1650.* Open May–Aug by appointment only. Buses 6, 84 & 86; tram 1 to Flórián tér.
Táborvárosi Múzeum (Roman Camp Museum), Aquincum. *Tel: (06 1) 250 1650.* See also pp34–5.
An excellent new publication in English detailing these sights is *Pannonia Hungaria Antiqua* (Archaeolingua).

Aquincum

The town originally existed to service the military – in every sense of the word. Including numerous brothels and pubs, the extensive rest-and-recreation area that surrounded the military *castrum* were collectively known as *canabae*.

At the beginning of the 2nd century Trajan enhanced Aquincum's status by making it the provincial capital of Pannonia Inferior. Hadrian raised it to a *municipium* in AD 124, and in 194, under Septimius Severus, it became a *colonia*. The Roman governor (*legatus*) established his residence on the adjacent Óbuda island.

Aquincum flourished in the 2nd and 3rd centuries, partly due to its proximity to the amber trade route that ran from the Baltic through western Hungary to Aquilea on the Adriatic. Decline set in during the 4th century, at the end of which Rome was forced to make concessions to the Huns and withdraw from the area.

Sights of Aquincum

Substantial ruins of Aquincum remain, indicating the prosperity of a city numbering 40,000 inhabitants who enjoyed the benefits of an efficient water supply, sewage disposal, and hypocaust heating. There were warm and cold baths and houses were decorated with frescoes, mosaics, and stucco. In the open-air part of the site are remnants of a forum, law courts, dwelling houses, and religious (including Christian) sanctuaries.

The museum contains everyday objects, either made locally or imported via the Rhine and the Danube from Germania and Gaul. Its star attraction is an organ worked by water pressure, a unique survival from Roman times.

Remains around Aquincum

South of the ruins is the so-called Herkules Villa, notable for mosaics depicting the labours of Hercules and Dionysian rites (wine production was encouraged in Pannonia from the 3rd century). One vivid scene shows Hercules about to loose an arrow at a centaur abducting a curvaceous nymph.

Nearby are the remains of a *cella trichora*, an early Christian chapel on a clover-leaf ground-plan. It dates to the 4th century and was probably built over a martyr's grave.

Just to the north of Aquincum are the remains of an aqueduct and of the civil amphitheatre, which is only half the size of the military one.

Ruins of Aquincum

Statues and Monuments

No free-standing monument from the Middle Ages has
survived in Budapest, and most of those of the Baroque
age have been taken to the Kiscelli Museum in order to
conserve them. The striking Baroque Trinity Column
(1713) on Szentháromság tér is an exception, but even this
is largely a post-war replica. It is one of the classic Buda
landmarks, on a spot where masses were held when plague
closed the churches.

Statue of Anonymous

Today, the visitor sees mainly 19th- and
20th-century statuary, the best of it
nobly commemorating men worthy of
honour, the worst of it (Socialist
Realism) now mostly consigned to the
new park of Communist monuments
near Nagytétény (*see pp102–3*).

Described here are monuments
of historical and/or aesthetic interest.
Many others are covered in the Walks or
in the descriptions of Kossuth Lajos tér
(*see p92*), Hősök tere (*see pp62–5*) or
Castle Hill, and the
Royal Palace (*see
pp48–53*).

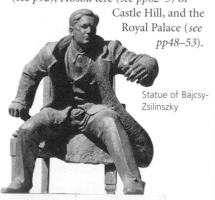
Statue of Bajcsy-
Zsilinszky

'SY-ZSILINSZKY ENDRE
1886-1944
'A HAZA MINDEN ELŐTT" KÖLCSEY

Anonymus Emlékmű
(Anonymous Monument)

This is understandably the capital's best-
loved monument (1903). The sculptor,
Miklós Ligeti, was the beneficiary of
money given by Emperor Wilhelm I of
Germany, who visited Budapest in 1897
and remarked on the need for more
statues in the city. He had in mind more
bombastic representations of warriors,
but the city authorities contented
themselves with a few muscle-bound
Turk-killers on Andrássy út. Ligeti's
subject is very different. Master P was
the anonymous monkish chronicler of
Béla III, and his *Gesta Hungarorum*
(1204) was the first history of the
Magyars. The sculptor has respected the
historian's anonymity by hiding his face
under his cowl.
Courtyard of Vajdahunyad Castle.
Metro: to Hősök tér.

Bajcsy-Zsilinszky Emlékmű
(Bajcsy-Zsilinszky Monument)

The dramatic sculpture (by Sándor
Győrfi, 1986) shows the politician who
headed the non-Communist resistance

to the Nazis at the moment of his arrest in Parliament by Hungarian fascists in 1944. He was shot shortly after his arrest. On the base of the monument is a quotation from Ferenc Kölcsey: '*A haza minden előtt*' ('the homeland before everything').
Deák Ferenc tér.
Metro: to Deák Ferenc tér.

Deák Emlékmű (Deák Monument)

Adolf Huszár's monument (1887) honours the lawyer and shrewd politician who was minister for justice in the independent government of 1848–9 and whose 'Easter Essay' in the *Pesti Napló* (16 April 1865) gave the impetus for the political Compromise of 1867 and the setting up of the Austro-Hungarian Dual Monarchy.

Ferenc Deák was a man of outstanding integrity, who lived for years as a bachelor in a suite of rooms in the nearby English Queen Hotel (the Gresham Palace was subsequently built on the site).
Roosevelt tér. Buses: 16 & 105.
Tram: 2 to Roosevelt tér.

Gellért Emlékmű (Gellért Monument)

On a dramatic site overlooking the Elizabeth Bridge rises the 6.76m bronze statue of Hungary's first missionary. Gyula Jankovics' work (1904) is supposedly situated near the spot where Gellért was either hurled to his death or rolled into the Danube, nailed inside a barrel (versions differ). St Gellért (Gerard Sagredo) was born in Venice around 980 and martyred in 1046. He tutored King Stephen's son, Emeric, and was made Bishop of Csanád by King Stephen in 1030.
Buses: 86, 5 & 78 to Szarvas tér.

St Gellért (Gerard Sagredo), first missionary to Hungary

Kodály Zoltán Szobor
(Statue of Zoltán Kodály)

In a grove on the northeast slopes of Castle Hill is Imre Varga's remarkable bronze (1982) of the composer Zoltán Kodály (1882–1967), which has been likened to 'pop art'. Varga is a prolific creator of modern public monuments, highly naturalistic, and often with a touch of humour.

Europapark. Várbusz: from Moszkva tér to Bécsi kapu tér.

József Nádor Emlékmű
(Palatine Joseph Monument)

Johann Halbig's elegant bronze figure (1869), draped in the cloak of St Stephen's Order, honours the younger brother of Emperor Franz I. Archduke Joseph (1776–1847) headed the Embellishment Commission (*see pp116–17*) that transformed the face of 19th-century Pest. He was one of the few Habsburgs to be loved by Hungarians.

Metro: to Deák Ferenc tér, then a short walk to Fozsef Nádor tér.

Raoul Wallenberg Emlékmű
(Raoul Wallenberg Monument)

Another bronze by Imre Varga (1987) is a belated tribute to the 'righteous Gentile' who saved thousands of Budapest Jews in 1944 by issuing them with Swedish identity cards. He probably died in a Russian gulag after the war.

Szilágyi Erzsébet fasor. Tram: 56 (four stops) from Moszkva tér.

Semmelweis Szobor
(Semmelweis Statue)

The marble statue (1906) of the 'Saviour of Mothers', Ignác Semmelweis (*see also p78*), is by Alajos Stróbl. The sculptor depicted his own wife and baby as part of the ensemble in recognition of the fact that Semmelweis's improvements in medical practice had saved their lives after a difficult birth.

Rochus Hospital, Gyulai Pál utca. Metro: to Blaha Lujza tér.

Szabadság Emlékmű
(Freedom Monument)

As soon as the Russians had 'liberated' Budapest (and Vienna) they hastened to erect monuments in prominent places so that a grateful public should keep their contribution permanently in mind the Freedom (formerly 'Liberation') Monument (1947) can be seen from most of Pest and much of Buda.

Ironically, Zsigmond Kisfaludy-Stróbl's work was originally intended to honour Admiral Horthy's son, a pilot killed in a crash thought to have been engineered by the Germans. The addition of a Soviet soldier holding the red flag and one or two other touches adroitly made the iconographical switch from Horthyism to Communism. The massive female figure holding aloft a palm branch is still there, but the Soviet soldier has gone

The symbol of freedom

The Great Synagogue

following the collapse of Communism.
*Gellért-hegy. Bus: 27 from Moricz
Zsigmond korter, Villanyi út to the stop
Busulo Juhasz, and then a 400m walk.*

Szoborpark (Sculpture Park)

The new home for the city's Communist
statuary (*see pp102–3*).
*Balatoni/corner Szabadkai út (22nd
District). Tel: (06 1) 424 7500;
www.szoborpark.hu
Open: daily 10am–dusk. Admission
charge. Trams: 19 & 49, or red bus 7 to
Etele tér, Kelenfoldi pályaudvar terminus.
Then yellow bus (every 5–30 min) to the
sculpture museum.*

SYNAGOGUES

Nagyzsinagóga (Great Synagogue)

The largest synagogue in Europe is still a
centre of liberal Judaism. It was built by
the Viennese architect Ludwig Förster
(1859) and enlarged in 1931 in Moorish
style, although the basilica-like ground
plan and a cloister-like arcade are

Christian in mood. Imre Varga's moving
Monument to the Holocaust Victims in
the rear courtyard recalls the terrible
events of the mid-20th century and
stands over the mass graves of
victims. The attached Zsidó Múzeum
(National Jewish Museum) is situated
where the founder of Zionism (Theodor
Herzl, 1860–1904) was born. It contains
disturbing documentation of Jewish
persecution.
*Dohány utca 2–8. Museum tel: (06 1) 342
8949; open: May–Oct, Mon–Thu 10am–
5pm, Fri 10am–3pm, Sun 10am–2pm;
Nov–Apr, Mon–Fri 10am–3pm, Sun
10am–1pm; closed: Sat.
Synagogue tel: (06 1) 342 1335;
open: Mon–Fri 10am–3pm, Sun
10am–1pm (except during ceremonies).
Closed: Sat. There are combined tickets
for the Synagogue and the museum.
Metro: to Astoria or Deák Ferenc tér.*

Zsinagóga (Orthodox Synagogue)

The rival to the liberal synagogue was
the (moderately) orthodox one, two
streets away, which also has a vividly
oriental look about it. The architect,
Otto Wagner, was later to become the
leading light of the Viennese Secession.
Currently, the synagogue is under
restoration and difficult to visit.
(*See p35.*)
*Rumbach Sebestyén utca 11–13.
Metro: to Astoria.*

Close by, in Dob utca, is a monument to
the Swiss Karl Lutz, in the form of an
angel stooping to help a fallen victim.
Like Wallenberg, Lutz helped Jews to
escape, although his method of buying
their freedom remains controversial.

Széchenyi Lánchíd
Széchenyi Chain Bridge

In 1820, a 29-year-old nobleman was returning hurriedly from Bihar County to Transdanubia for the funeral of his father. He reached Pest on 29 December, only to find that the pontoon bridge over the Danube had been dismantled for three weeks. It was not until 5 January of 1821 that he could persuade a ferryman to negotiate the treacherous ice-floes. The nobleman was Count István Széchenyi and his reaction to this experience was to begin lobbying vigorously for the building of a long-mooted bridge between Pest and Buda.

On 10 February, 1832, the Budapest Bridge Association was formed under Széchenyi's chairmanship. Following an old Central European tradition, it included not only enthusiasts, but also those who would otherwise have stymied the project out of jealousy, had they not been included.

Opposition came from the municipalities, who were unwilling to forgo the revenue of the pontoon toll, and from the nobility, who clung to their privilege of toll exemption which the owners of a privately built bridge were no longer prepared to indulge. However, the enlightened Palatine, Joseph, supported the project and the resistance of the aristocrats was finally overcome.

Looking through the famous triumphal arches

COUNT ISTVÁN SZÉCHENYI (1791–1860)

Called 'the greatest Hungarian' by his political rival, Lajos Kossuth, Széchenyi was a reformer, a patriot, and an enthusiast for technical innovation. He donated one year's income from his estates towards the foundation of the Academy of Sciences in 1827, and founded, *inter alia,* the National Theatre, the Danube Steamship Company, and the Óbuda shipyard. He also organised the regulation of the Danube and the Tisza, and improved the quality of Hungarian livestock.

Although he served briefly as transport minister in the independent government of 1848, his last days were clouded by mental instability. In 1860 he committed suicide in a Vienna sanatorium. His words sum up his political and social attitudes: 'We must struggle for the general good, as well as our own interest.'

he Chain Bridge – the first to link Pest and Buda

Széchenyi travelled to England to study bridge-building. He was impressed by William Tierney Clark's suspension bridge at Marlow in Buckinghamshire, and Clark was invited to design the Budapest Bridge. A Scottish master-builder, Adam Clark (no relation), was engaged for the work. The project was jointly financed by Viennese bankers (Georg Sina, Samuel Wodianer, and Jakob Rothschild). Construction (1842–8) was not without difficulties: as the last component was being lowered into position, the chain of the hoist snapped, demolishing part of the scaffolding and pitching onlookers (including Széchenyi) into the Danube.

The Chain Bridge was completed just before the outbreak of the War of Independence and survived an attempt by the Austrians to blow it up. It was officially inaugurated after the war (by which time Széchenyi was confined to a Viennese mental asylum). Its imposing triumphal arches instantly became Budapest's most characteristic land-mark, but the sculpted lions by János Marschalkó were criticised for apparently lacking tongues. The sculptor was able to demonstrate in several learned articles that lions' tongues 'do not hang out of the mouth like those of dogs'.

The city had given an undertaking to the construction company not to build a competing bridge either side of the Chain Bridge closer than a distance of 8km. Pressure of traffic soon made this condition intolerable and in 1870 the municipality bought the company out, so that construction of the Margaret Bridge could begin.

The Communists stamped their presence all over Budapest in the form of street names and monuments, and newly elected city councils have been assiduous in removing these since the toppling of the regime in 1989.

Scores of names have been changed. Many were obvious candidates for oblivion – Engels Square or Lenin Avenue, for instance. Some were names associated with the obsessive Communist quest for legitimacy (Liberation Square,

People's Army Square, First of May Avenue); others immortalised little-known minor functionaries.

In the autumn of 1992 work began on the removal (at huge cost) of 56 Communist statues from squares and parks, spurred on by activists of the Hungarian Association of Freedom Fighters of 1956. They announced that, if any were left *in situ* on 23 October (the anniversary of the 1956 revolution), they would tear them down with their own hands – a fate which befell the mega-statue of Stalin during the revolution itself.

Many of the Socialist Realist sculptures have been placed in a specially built park outside Budapest, Szoborpark – a 'Disneyland of old Communism' as the deputy mayor described it. The presentation is dramatic: as you walk through a pedimented gateway flanked by larger than life statues of Lenin, Marx, and Engels, a vista opens before you of heroically depicted groups of toiling workers or fighting soldiers, powerfully evoking the mixture of ideology and kitsch that passed for Communist art. In the view of the deputy mayor their preservation is itself an assertion of civilised values.

Meanwhile someone has discovered a warehouse full of Habsburg monuments that miraculously survived destruction in the 1950s. There are, of course, spaces for these now. . .

For location and details see p99.

www.szoborpark.hu

Statues of Communist heroes relegated to the Sculpture Park near Nagytétény

Váci Utca (Vác Street)

Váci utca used to be two streets (it incorporated Lipót utca at the beginning of the 18th century) and they were quite different. However, the southern part, formerly decayed, has been transformed to resemble the pedestrian zone of the northern half. The latter has been likened to shopping malls such as Kärntner Strasse in Vienna or even London's Bond Street. It was always a fashionable promenade, as 19th-century etchings show, but most of its fine Neo-Classical buildings have disappeared.

Number 9 is the Pest Theatre, built by József Hild in 1840 on the site of a famous hotel and ballroom where the 11-year-old prodigy, Franz Liszt, once gave a concert. Number 11a is faced with colourful Zsolnay ceramics and was built in the Jugendstil style by Ödön Lechner and Gyula Pártos (1890). Also worth a glance is the Post-Modern Taverna Hotel (No. 20) by József Finta and Associates (1987), which is complemented by the same partnership's International Trade Centre opposite.

Váci utca seems to be awash with people night and day. There are Transylvanian ladies selling their fine embroidery, and stalls offering city guides, fragrance therapy, acacia honey, and much else. *Metro: to Ferenciek tere or Vörösmarty tér.*

Vígszínház (Comedy Theatre)

The charming Neo-Rococo theatre was built by the Viennese firm of Fellner and Helmer. When it opened in 1896, the public were sceptical of its chances of survival (it was too far out from the centre and had no funding from the state). In fact, a diet of Hungarian and European comedies, played in naturalistic style, soon had audiences

A beautiful example of an old street lamp

The statue of Mihály Vörösmarty

FERENC MOLNÁR 1878–1952

Molnár made a career on Broadway as well as in his native Pest and is the best-known Hungarian dramatist abroad. His polished and witty comedies are full of psychological insight and erotic innuendo. The Rodgers and Hammerstein musical *Carousel* was based on his play *Liliom* (1909), a low-life story set in the amusement arcade of the City Woodland Park in Pest. Asked how he became a writer, he replied: 'In the same way a woman becomes a prostitute. First I did it to please myself, then I did it to please my friends, and finally I did it for money'.

flocking to it. Ferenc Molnár was one who began his career here. Between the wars the staging of modern playwrights' work and visits by guest companies from abroad built up the theatre's reputation.

Szent István körút 14. Tel: (061) 370 4650. Buses: 6, 15, 26, 91, 191; trams 4 & 6.

Vörösmarty Tér (Vörösmarty Square)

The spacious square is entered from Váci utca at a point where the inner city gate for the road to Vác (*see p132*) once stood. Under the trees in the centre is a monument of Carrara marble (by Ede Telcs and Ede Kallós, 1908) to the Romantic poet Mihály Vörösmarty (1800–55). The poet is shown reciting his *Szózat* (Appeal) to the Hungarian masses; etched on the plinth is a line

from the poem: 'Be faithful to your land forever, O Hungarians!' Although *Szózat* contains more optimistic passages, the nightmare vision it evoked of *'nemzethalál'* (national extinction) spoke directly to the hearts of Hungarians, then as now.

On the north side of the square is a block built by József Hild, long known as the 'cutters' house' because a wealthy tailor, a surgeon, a slaughterer, and a banker lived here (presumably the banker was seen as someone who could cut off the money supply). On the ground floor is the celebrated café and confectioner's, Gerbeaud (*see p170*). *Metro: to Vörösmarty tér. The main Tourinform Office (open daily 24 hrs) along with police assistance for tourists is here. Entrance at Vigadó utca 6, side street.*

Váci utca, fashionable shopping district

(pork in aspic), *szalonna* (bacon), and *zsír* (lard).

For centuries Hungary was an agrarian feudal society, and many a city dweller is still provided by country cousins with home-made fare, vegetables, and fruit. A popular 'rustic' tradition among young Budapestians today is the *szalonnasütés* (bacon barbecue). In a suitably rural environment, such as Szentendre Island, bacon is roasted with peppers and potatoes, and Magyar folk songs are sung.

A more genuine peasant tradition is the December *disznóölés* (pig-killing); every part of the pig is used to make *kolbász* (sausage), *hurka* (black pudding), *sonka* (ham), *disznósajt* (pickled feet and ears), *kocsonya*

While life in the country is still geared to the rhythm of the seasons, urban Hungarians often juggle their waking hours between two jobs in order to make ends meet. Life is hectic; by Western standards it is also uncomfortable for most, due to a perennial shortage of accommodation. Young married couples are often condemned to live with in-laws, and most families have bedrooms that double as sitting-rooms. In the inner city, many live in hideous concrete 'panel-housing' blocks, notorious for tacky quality and lack of privacy. In the suburbs, life is more agreeable for those who live in family bungalows with lovingly tended vegetable gardens. Suburbanites may keep fit by gardening, but city dwellers must turn to other means. Swimming in the spas is a popular pastime, combining as it does opportunities for gossip with healthy exercise. At summer weekends most of Budapest flees to Lake Balaton, where many people have built holiday homes.

More space,

more cash, and more attention to diet are beginning to have an impact on Hungarian lifestyle. Unlikely to change are the gregarious habits of the Magyars, their capacity to make much out of little, and their ability to fill the calendar with excuses for celebration. Every day, it seems, is somebody's name day, and therefore an excuse for a visit that begins with the enigmatic greeting: *'Isten éltessen sokáig/a füled érjen bokáig'* ('May God grant you a long life and may your ears reach your ankles').

The joys of eating, drinking, and lazing, while some earn their living by playing music on the streets

Várhegy

Castle Hill

The wedge-shaped limestone plateau rising 160m on the west side of the Danube consists of the Royal Castle complex (*see pp48–53*) at the southern end and the ancient town of Buda (the Várhegyed or Castle Quarter), encompassing the middle and northern parts of the plateau.

Attractive boutiques and a bookshop are to be found in the Fortuna Passage

From the time of Béla IV in the 13th century, old Buda was a residential area ancillary to the court, where retainers, officials, craftsmen, and merchants lived (*see pp24–5*). Each component of its mixed population of Germans and Hungarians (also Walloons, Italians, and Jews) has left traces here; even the last Turkish pasha has his monument, although there is very little else left to recall the 146-year-long Turkish rule. After the Diet ceased to meet in Buda at the beginning of the 19th century, Pest increasingly eclipsed Buda, until it gradually became the quiet backwater of today.

Access to Várhegy

Whether you want to visit the Royal Palace, the town, or both, the following access routes will apply: from the south the approach is on foot from Szarvas tér (reached by bus 86 on the Buda side, bus 5 and 78 from Pest) and brings you through the southern fortifications of the old castle. There are also various flights of steps up from Fő utca in Víziváros (Water Town). The buses from Pest to

Gates to the former Royal Palace

Dísz tér on the southern end of the Castle Quarter are No. 16 from Erzsébet tér (Deák ferenc tér metro). The *sikló* (funicular) climbs from Clark Ádám tér at the west end of the Chain Bridge (daily 7.30am–10pm) and arrives at Szent György tér (there is a special fare for this). The *várbusz* (minibus) runs between Szent György tér and Moszkva tér (metro red line) until mid-evening; it stops at strategic points in Buda town (city tickets and passes valid).

Bécsi Kapu Tér (Vienna Gate Square)

To the left of the gate are the sombre State Archives and opposite it is the Lutheran Church containing Bertalan Székely's picture, *Christ Blessing the Bread*. There are attractive Baroque houses at Nos 5 and 6, and the façade of No. 7 is adorned with medallions of Virgil, Socrates, Quintillian, Cicero, Livy, and Seneca.

Dísz Tér (Parade Square)

The square is flanked by the Water Gate to the east and the Fehérvári or Jewish Gate to the west; to the south are the ruins of the War Ministry. Jews were settled close to the castle by Béla IV and held a Friday market here, until driven out by Louis of Anjou in 1360. Executions (a popular spectacle) were held on the square. In the middle is György Zala's *Honvéd Monument* (1893), honouring Hungarians who died for freedom in 1848–9.

Fortuna Utca (Fortuna Street)

French and Walloon craftsmen lived in the street in the Middle Ages. Gothic elements can be seen in several houses,

Fishermen's Bastion

notably the so-called *sedilia* (sitting niches) in the doorways (for example, at No. 5), a unique feature of Buda. They may have been used by traders for their wares or by servants waiting for their masters. At No. 4 is the Museum of Commerce and Catering (*see p76*).

Halászbástya (Fishermen's Bastion)

Frigyes Schulek designed this Neo-Romanesque viewing terrace to the east and south of the Mátyás templom (Matthias Church); completed in 1905, it was named after the Danube fishermen who defended this bastion in the Middle Ages. The conical turrets are supposedly a romantic allusion to the tents of the original Magyar tribes. In front of the bastion is Alajos Stróbl's equestrian statue of St Stephen (1903) holding the (doubled) Apostolic Cross that symbolises his role as Christianiser of the Hungarians.

Hess András Tér (András Hess Square)

The square is named after the printer of the first Hungarian book, *Budai krónika* (The Chronicle of Buda, 1473) – his printing shop was at No. 4. The Hilton Hotel (Nos 1–2) is a modern adaptation of a former Dominican monastery and church. On the St Nicholas Tower of the former church is a copy of a 15th-century Saxon relief showing a triumphant King Matthias. Also on the square is the monument to Pope Innocent XI, initiator of the Holy Alliance formed to reconquer Buda from the Turks.

Kapisztrán Tér (Giovanni Capistrano Square)

Capistrano was a fiery Franciscan preacher who gathered an army against the Turks and took part in the successful siege of Belgrade in 1456. Appropriately, the Museum of Military History is also on the square (Nos 2–4, *see p72*). On the Anjou Bastion beyond it is the monument to the last pasha of Buda, Abdurrahman Abdi Arnaut (actually an Albanian), who died at his post in 1686.

Magdolna Templom (Church of St Mary Magdalene)

The tower and a solitary Gothic window of the choir are all that has been reconstructed after wartime bombardment of the church. It belonged to the Hungarians in the Middle Ages; after prolonged dispute a borderline between the German and Hungarian parishes had been drawn at the Dominican Monastery (now the Hilton) in 1390. Under the Turkish occupation the church was for a while shared between Protestants (worshipping in the nave) and Catholics (using the choir). *Kapisztrán tér.*

HISTORY OF THE MATTHIAS CHURCH

The earliest church on this site dates back to the reign of Béla IV (1235–70). It was enlarged in the late 14th century, and subsequently add to by Matthias Corvinus, who built the oratory and replaced the south tower that had collapsed in 1384.

During the Turkish occupation, it was used as a mosque. Then, between 1874 and 1896, Frigyes Schulek entirely rebuilt it in Neo-Gothic style though he stuck to the original ground-plan.

The Church of Our Lady in the Middle Ages was where the German burghers of Buda held their services. The kings of Hungary had to be formally accepted by the community in the church following their coronation in Székesfehérvár.

After the Compromise of 1867, Franz Joseph and Elizabeth were crowned in this church, as were the last Habsburgs, Karl IV and Zita, in 1916.

Church of St Mary Magdalene

Mátyás Templom (Matthias Church)

The Church of Our Lady is known as the Matthias Church after King Matthias Corvinus (1458–90), who considerably enlarged and enriched it. The interior was painted with polychrome geometric patterns and frescoes in the 19th century by Károly Lotz and Bertalan Székely; the stained-glass windows show scenes from Hungarian history.

Against the north wall of the choir is the St Ladislas Chapel with a copy of the 14th-century silver bust of the 11th-century saint and king, Ladislas I, and frescoes by Lotz, illustrating legends about him. In the crypt are grave slabs of the Árpád dynasty. From there, you begin a tour which includes St Stephen's Chapel, painted with scenes from the life of the saint-king, the Royal Oratory (containing Habsburg coronation robes), and the exhibition of ecclesiastical treasures in the north gallery. Below it, in the Trinity Chapel, is the tomb of Béla III and his consort, Anne of Châtillon. *Szentháromság tér 2. Tel: (06 1) 355 5657. Open: 7am–8pm (for groups Mon–Sat 9am–6pm, Sun 1–5pm). English speaking guides available. Admission charge (also for gift shop).*

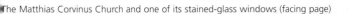

The Matthias Corvinus Church and one of its stained-glass windows (facing page)

Athena guards the old Town Hall, Trinity Square

Országház Utca
(The Street of the Diet)

The Italian craftsmen working on the Royal Palace once lived in this street (it was then called 'Olasz utca' – Italian Street). From the 1780s to 1807 the Hungarian Diet met at No. 28, formerly a convent. Of the many attractive survivals, Nos 18–22 retain Gothic and Baroque features, while No. 2 was a place of some splendour at the time of Sigismund of Luxembourg (note the sitting niches).

Sándor Palota (Sándor Palace)

Mihály Pollack and the Viennese Johann Aman designed this imposing Neo-Classical palace (1805–1821). It was the official lodging of the prime minister between 1867 and 1944 (*see p114*). Note Anton Kirchmayer's frieze on the façade, a mixture of patriotic themes and scenes from antiquity.

Szent György tér 1–2. The palace is undergoing renovation for government use and is closed to visitors.

Szentháromság Tér (Trinity Square)

Trinity Square is the focus of the old town: to the east is the Matthias Church (*see p111*), to the north, the Neo-Gothic Central Archive (formerly the Finance Ministry), and to the west, the Régi budai városháza (Old Town Hall). This Baroque fusion of five Gothic houses was seat of the council from 1710 to 1873. Szentháromság utca leads off to the west; at No. 7 is the Biedermeier café Ruszwurm (*see p171*). In the middle of the square is the Trinity Column (1713) commemorating the abatement of a plague epidemic.

Táncsics Mihály Utca
(Mihály Táncsics Street)

At No. 7 is the Baroque Erdődy Palace

1769) housing the Museum of the History of Music (*see p77*). Number 9 may once have been the royal mint; it certainly became the Magna Curia (Royal Court) and was latterly a prison. The writer and agitator Mihály Táncsics was imprisoned here before the War of Independence. The Jewish ghetto was around Nos 21 and 23. Number 26, formerly a synagogue, is now a museum. A wall plan shows the location of Buda's Jewish community at various periods. Dependent on the goodwill of the ruler, they suffered periodic persecution or expulsion. The Christian armies that reconquered Buda in 1686 massacred the Jewish inhabitants, who had established a *modus vivendi* with the Turks.

Synagogue museum: Tancsics utca 23 & 26. Tel: (06 1) 355 8849. Open: 10am–6pm. Closed: Nov–Apr.

Tárnok Utca (Treasurers' Street)

The name refers to the administrators of the royal monopolies (salt, minerals, etc) who resided in the area. The street was also the site of a market in the Middle Ages. No. 18 is a medieval building converted to a Baroque apothecary's shop, now a museum with a display of utensils and period fittings.

Arany Sas Patikamúzeum – Golden Eagle Museum, Tárnok utca 18. Tel: (06 1) 375 9772. Open: Tue–Sun 10.30am–5.30pm.

Úri Utca (The Street of the Lords)

At No. 9 is the entrance to the cave labyrinth under Castle Hill (*see p134*), while at the junction with Szentháromság utca is an equestrian statue of Maria Theresa's successful Hungarian general, András Hadik, who was also commandant of Buda for a while. His horse is a portrait of a famous stallion from the stud at Bábolna.

Várszínház (Castle Theatre)

Originally a 13th-century Franciscan monastery, the building was occupied by the Turkish pashas between 1541 and 1686. It was turned into a German theatre in 1787 and saw the first ever Hungarian stage performance in the city on 25 October 1790.

Színház utca 5–9. Tel: (06 1) 356 4085.

Trinity Column and the Neo-Gothic Central Archive, Trinity Square

Walk: Várhegy

This walk round Castle Hill gives a flavour of the old town of Buda, painstakingly restored after terrible destruction in World War II.

Allow 1½ hours.

Start from the top of the funicular railway (sikló), also the Várbusz terminal, that climbs to Castle Hill from Clark Ádám tér.

1 Sándor-Palota (Sandor Palace)

On your right is the beautifully restored Neo-Classical former prime minister's residence (*see p112*). A plaque on the east wall honours Count Teleki, head of the government in 1941, who committed suicide here when the decision was taken to allow German troops through Hungary to attack Yugoslavia.

2 Várszínház (Castle Theatre)

The former monastery was converted into a theatre (*see p113*) by the engineer

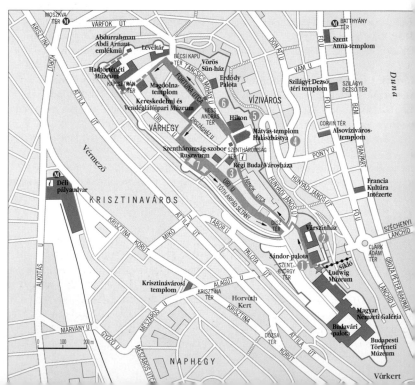

Farkas Kempelen, inventor of a 'speaking machine' and an 'automatic chess player' that once defeated Napoleon (it actually concealed a diminutive chess genius inside).
Walk through Dísz tér and Tárnok utca to Szentháromság tér.

Régi Budai Városháza (Former Town Hall of Buda)

The early-18th century town hall on the west side of the square has a pretty bay window; below it is a statue of Pallas Athene, protectress of Buda. A clock tower with an onion dome rises from an upper-storey Baroque chapel, dedicated to St John the Almsgiver (c.560–619).

Mátyás Templom, Halászbástya (Matthias Church, Fishermen's Bastion)

The striking Neo-Gothic reconstruction of the Matthias Church (*see p111*) dominates the square's east side. If it looks a bit like a stage-set, the Fishermen's Bastion beyond it (by the same architect, *see p109*) looks even more so.

5 Hilton Hotel

Further north, the Hilton Hotel (1976) at Hess András tér 4 was ingeniously designed by Béla Pintér, incorporating the base of a medieval tower (now a casino), the remains of a Gothic church, and a late Baroque seminary.

A detour down Táncsics Mihály utca brings you past the Erdődy Palota (No. 7) containing the Museum of the History of Music; next door (No. 9) is where leading dissidents were imprisoned before the anti-Habsburg revolution of 1848.

6 Hess András Tér/Fortuna Utca

At No. 3 on the square is the ancient Vörös Sün-ház (House of the Red Hedgehog – see the relief above the door).

Turn left at No. 4 for the Litea bookshop/café and boutiques. Inside the Baroque house at No. 4 Fortuna utca is the Kereskedelmi és Vendéglátóipari Múzeum (Museum of Commerce and Catering, *see p76*).

It is worth a detour on to the Anjou bastion to see the monument to the last Turkish pasha (Abdurrahman Abdi Arnaut emlékmű, *see p110*). Walk back across Kapisztrán tér to Országház utca, leaving the stunted remains of the Magdolna templom (Church of St Mary Magdalene on your right, *see p110*). On the corner with Petermann bíró utca, note the modern wall plaque of 'The Flying Nun'. It recalls the convent of the Poor Clares at Országház utca 28, later the seat of the Hungarian Diet.
Cut through Dárda utca and head south along Úri utca, where there are unusual Gothic sitting niches in the entrance to Nos 31, 32 & 34. After catching the view over the Krisztinaváros from the west rampart (Tóth Árpád sétány), turn left by the equestrian statue to András Hadik (see p113) into Szentháromság utca.

7 Ruszwurm

At No. 7 is the famous confectioner's (*see p171*). In the late 19th century, Vilmos Ruszwurm's pastries were in such demand that well-to-do Viennese ordered them to be sent by post-chaise.
Turn south out of the street for Dísz tér for buses to Pest; and the várbusz to Moszkva tér.

Városliget
City Woodland Park

The 1-km square Városliget is a playground for Budapestians, young and old, an historic landmark, and a veritable paradise for lovers of trees, of which the park has over 6,900, including several rare species. The area was once a hostile swamp through which meandered the stagnant waters of the Rákos Creek.

Vajdahunyad Castle

In 1240, the Tatar army of Batu Khan inflicted a crushing defeat on the Magyars here by feigning a retreat and luring their opponents on to the marsh. In 1259, Béla IV granted what had now become pastureland, known as the *ukur* (ox land) to the Dominicans of Margaret Island.

The sandy meadows were annexed to Pest by Leopold I, and Maria Theresa instigated systematic tree planting in 1751. The Embellishment Commission of the city further improved the park, after holding a competition (won by a Bavarian landscape gardener, Henrik Nebbien) for the best ideas to beautify it.

The Embellishment Commission
The popular Palatine,
Joseph, threw his weight behind an imaginative 26-point plan for improving and beautifying Pest according to a proposal by the architect János Hild. A commission set up to realise Hild's ideas first met in November 1808. Its primary business was urban planning to integrate the city core with fast-developing new districts. The Commission laid down regulations concerning the maximum height of houses and their exterior decoration. It was these that subsequently determined the unified aspect of Neo-Classical Pest. The Commission also gave its attention to the greening of the city through tree-planting and landscaping of Margaret Island and the City Woodland Park.

The ever-increasing

JÁNOS HUNYADI
(c.1407–56)

János Hunyadi was Hungary's greatest general in the early wars against the Turks, and the father of King Matthias Corvinus. He was Regent between 1446 and 1453.

Hunyadi rose to prominence at the court of King Sigismund, whose illegitimate son he was rumoured to be. His greatest triumph was at Nándorfehérvár (Belgrade) in 1456, a battle that stopped the Turkish advance for 70 years. To mark this victory Pope Calixtus III ordered the church bells of Christendom to be rung each day at noon in perpetuity.

inancial burden it placed on citizens, who had to pay for the projects, ontributed to the Commission's decline fter 1830 and it was finally dissolved in 856. In 1870, it was succeeded by the ighly successful Council of Public Vorks, which planned the next and reatest phase of city expansion.

The park contains several sights and nuseums covered on other pages: the zéchenyi baths (*see p37*), the Museum f Transport (*see p73*), the Agricultural Museum (*see p76*), the Amusement 'ark, and the Zoo (*see p155*).

ajdahunyad Vára
Vajdahunyad Castle)

)ne of the most popular features of the 896 Millennial exhibition held in the ity Woodland Park was Ignác Alpár's rchitectural phantasmagoria, originally temporary structure, but by popular lemand, it was subsequently rebuilt in

stone (1904–8). It presented a stylistic cross-section of architecture in Hungary through the ages. The Romanesque is represented by a replica of its best preserved example, the cathedral at Ják in western Hungary, and the Baroque by the somewhat heavy Neo-Baroque of the Agricultural Museum. The *pièce de résistance*, however, is the Vajdahunyad Castle, which gave its name to the whole complex (its famous original was the seat of the Hunyadi clan in Transylvania). Additional Gothic and Renaissance sections copied from other buildings create a bizarre Hollywood effect, so that you half expect Errol Flynn to jump out of a castle window. In the courtyard is Miklós Ligeti's (*see p96*) fine statue of Béla III's chronicler. The castle replica itself is one-third of the size of the original in Romania.
Városliget is reached by metro to Hősök tere or Széchenyi fürdő.

hess in Városliget

Views of the City

One of the joys of Budapest is that it can be viewed from so many different vantage points. Summer or winter, wind, rain, snow, or sunshine, all create different moods and stress different aspects of the city.

Looking out over the city

VIEWS FROM BUDA
Várhegy (Castle Hill)
Castle Hill is ringed by bastions. Those

on the northern and western sides have been turned into pleasant promenades. Views of the Vérmező (*see p59*) and the

Budapest Environs

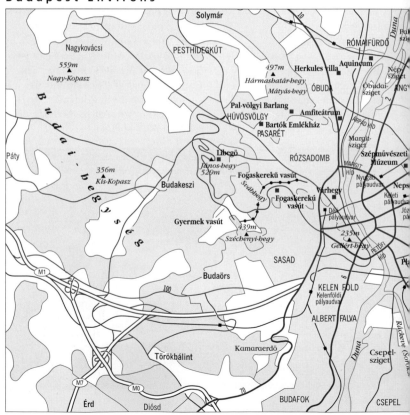

residential quarter, Krisztinaváros, can be enjoyed from the chestnut-shaded Tóth Árpád sétány.

On the other side of the hill you can see the parliament from Frigyes Schulek's Fishermen's Bastion (*see* p109). Further along the rim of Castle Hill to the south are excellent views from the terraces in front of the Castle Theatre and National Gallery. *Castle Hill districts can be reached by the várbusz from Moszkva tér.*

Gellért-hegy (Gellért Hill)

For dramatic views over the central and southern purlieus of the city and downstream Danube the best vantage points are from Gellért Hill.

Bus: 27 from Móricz Zsigmond körtér to Villányi út to the stop Búsuló Juhász, then a 400m walk.

Budai-hegység (Buda Hills)

Just beyond Rózsadomb (Hill of Roses) is the now rather dilapidated lookout tower on József-hegy, with one of the best upstream views of the Danube (take bus 191 from Nyugati pályaudvar to the end stop – Sarolta utca). The Árpád-torony on Látó-hegy (bus 11 from Batthyány tér to end stop)is one of the loveliest spots in the city.

The Hármashatár, Szabadság, and Széchenyi hills all offer attractive vistas. The highest Buda hill, János-hegy (529m), which can be reached by bus 21 from Moszkva tér metro; from the end of the line walk through the forest. (You can also take the chairlift from Zugliget, terminal of bus 158 from Moszkva tér). On the summit is the celebrated Erzsébet-torony (1910), named after Queen Elizabeth. Frigyes Schulek's tower has four levels of viewing platforms.

VIEWS FROM PEST

The fashionable Duna-korzó (the promenade between Chain Bridge and Elizabeth Bridge) offers the best views of the Royal Castle and Castle Hill (on UNESCO's World Heritage List). For a vista of Pest from an unusual angle, climb the cupola of St Stephen's Basilica (*see p56*) – but be warned: there are over 300 steps!

A City and its River

The Danube is the second longest river in Europe after the Volga: the Széchenyi Lánchíd (Chain Bridge) in Budapest is not yet half way along its 2,820km course. On the Budapest stretch it is generally around 5m deep, although there are some holes near Szabadság híd where it plunges to 8 or 9m. The bed is pebbles, loam, and sand with outcrops of rock. The flood period is in June, and lowest water levels are reached in October and December.

In Roman times the river was the furthest boundary of the empire and, with its chain of fortresses (*limes*), a formidable barrier to threatening tribes from the east. Thereafter, its greatest value was as a trade route – the 'dustless highway' in a chronicler's picturesque phrase. Goods had to be dragged upstream with teams of horses – or convicts where the bank was too treacherous for animals.

Things changed when the first steamship arrived in 1818. The journey from Pest to Vienna was cut from a month to three days and Hungarian agricultural exports boomed. The importance of Pest as a port was underlined by the scale of Miklós Ybl's imposing Customs House (1874 – now the University of Economics). In the 20th century, a free port was built on the edge of Csepel Island.

Until regulation in the 1870s, floods were a recurring hazard (there were 12 major ones between 1732 and 1838). To improve matters, the main channel was made deeper and narrower, and land was drained along the banks. Both the Parliament and the Technical University were built on reclaimed land. Floods are unlikely to occur nowadays, but to make sure they don't, ice-

breakers are deployed in winter. The bigger problem now is low water, which sometimes forces suspension of shipping.

During World War II all Budapest's bridges were destroyed, making ferries indispensible to cross-river traffic. Only one ferry operates today, in the northeastern part of the city, for use only by people, not vehicles. The Danube is now crossed by 10 bridges (2 railway and 8 pedestrian). The red metro line also crosses it between parliament and the Batthyány tér.

Today's Danube is a largely tamed creature, the haunt of scullers and canoeists, and a few optimistic anglers on the lookout for some of the 51 species of fish reputed to reside in its grey (seldom blue) waters. Still, the river is the artery of Hungary, inextricably bound up with the nation's history. (See pp40–41.)

Everyday scenes along the Danube

Excursions

LAKE BALATON

One hundred kilometres southwest of Budapest is Lake Balaton, Central Europe's largest inland sea with a shoreline of 200km, a surface area of 595sq km, and an average depth of no more than 2m. Its warm waters (30°C in summer) make it Hungary's most popular resort. Sailing, windsurfing, and horse-riding are additional attractions, as is fishing: there are 40 different species of fish in the lake, the most famous being the indigenous *fogas* (pike-perch).

Tihany

The Benedictine abbey of Tihany is situated on a basalt promontory overhanging the deepest part of the lake. It was founded by Andrew I in 1055 and its Baroque church contains beautiful carving by Sebestyén Stulhoff. The ample-bosomed angel on the Altar of the Virgin Mary is supposed to be a portrait of the artist's beloved, a local fisherman's daughter. The Romanesque crypt contains the simple gravestone of King Andrew, who died in 1060.

Local handicrafts on show

The delightful country house of Keszthely

Other sights of interest include the Abbey Museum, in the former priory. The display covers local topography and the origins of the Magyars; one room is devoted to the physicist Lóránd Eötvös (1849–1919), who conducted experiments on the Balaton ice-pack. The rustically furnished House of the Fishermen's Guild, off Pinsky Promenade, has material on the life of the Balaton fishermen. To the north is the Visszhangdomb (Echo Hill), and beyond that the Óvar (old earthern castle ruin). In its rock base Orthodox monks carved out their hermit cells. *Hourly buses run from Balatonfüred railway station. For bus timetable, see www.balatonvolan.hu www.menetrendek.hu*

Badacsony

A little further west is the table-top volcanic mountain of Badacsony. Its vine-clad slopes produce some of the region's best wines, notably *Szürkebarát* (Pinot Gris). The southeastern face has impressive basalt columns over 50m high. In the town centre, just north of the main road, is the József Egry Memorial Museum, devoted to the Balaton's famous local painters.

Keszthely

At the lake's western end is the town of Keszthely, 190km from Budapest, with the Festetics country mansion. Count György Festetics (1755–1819) lived here in 'retirement' (semi-exile) after taking part in a failed rebellion against the Habsburgs. While here, he founded the Helikon circle of reform-minded intellectuals and an agricultural university known as the Georgikon. The high point of the tour of the interior is the Helikon Library, beautifully constructed from Slavonian oak by a local carpenter. In the town, the Balaton Museum covers zoological, ethnological, and archaeological aspects of the region. There are also wine and marzipan museums (*see www.keszthely.hu*).

Other Places of Interest

At the lake's east end the spa of Balatonfüred has charm. Hévíz (8km from Keszthely) is a thermal lake fed by a source 1km below the surface (the baths are open 7am–4pm). The marshy Kis-Balaton at the lake's western tip, where the River Zala runs into it, is good territory for birdwatchers. Along the southern shore there are many

Vines at Badacsony

resorts, of which Siófok is the biggest and most popular with the younger set.

Lake Balaton is 100km southwest of Budapest. The best way to reach is by InterCity trains which require reservation (well in advance in summer). See Thomas Cook European Timetable *for times. Trains leave from Déli pályaudvar (Southern Railway Station).*

Balaton Museum Múzeum utca 2, Keszthely. *Tel: (06 83) 312 351.* Open: Tue–Sun 10am–6pm (Oct–Apr, Tue–Sat 9am–5pm).
Festetics Country Mansion Kastély utca 1, Keszthely. *Tel: (06 83) 312 191; www.keszthely.hu* Open: daily 9am–5pm (until 6pm in Jul & Aug).
József Egry Memorial Museum Egry sétány 12, Badacsony. *Tel: (06 87) 431 044; www.c3.hu/~vmmuzeum* Open: May–Sep, Tue–Sun 10am–6pm.
Tihany Abbey Museum 1 Andras tér 1 *Tel: (06 87) 448 650; www.tihany.hu* Open: May–Sep, Tue–Sun 10am–5pm.

DUNAKANYAR
(The Danube Bend)

The Danube enters Hungary flowing west to east, but after Esztergom it is forced into an S-shape in a narrow valley between the Pilis and Börzsöny Mountains. After Visegrád it completes a final loop, thereafter settling on a north–south course. This whole stretch of the river – from Esztergom to Szentendre Island – is known as the Danube Bend, an area of enchantingly dramatic scenery.

Esztergom

Esztergom is where King Stephen was born (c.975) and where he was crowned on Christmas Day, 1000. He founded Esztergom's archbishopric the following year; Hungarian Primates were based here until the Turkish conquest and returned only in the 19th century.

The Basilica in Esztergom

Esztergom is 64km from Budapest on Road 11. Half-hourly buses from Árpád híd (Pest side). Trains from Nyugati pályaudvar. A boat leaves at 7.30am on summer weekends from Vigadó tér, Budapest.

The Basilica

Hungary's largest church, begun in 1822 and completed in 1869, is more imposing than pleasing, but do not miss (to the left inside) the red marble funerary chapel (1507) of Archbishop Tamás Bakócz, a relic of the original cathedral here. The crypt contains some fine Renaissance sarcophagi and the *kincstár* (Treasury) has exquisite gold and silversmiths' work.
Szent István tér 1. Tel: (06 33) 411 895.
Open: Mar–Dec, daily 9am–5pm;
Jan–Feb, Tue–Sun 7am–4pm.
Treasury tel: (06 33) 402 354.
Open: Mar–Sep, daily 9am–4.30pm;
Oct–Dec 11am–4pm. Closed: Jan.
Admission charge.

Vármúzeum (Medieval Royal Castle)

The old castle is just to the south of the basilica. It includes a 12th-century chapel with a fine rose window, the Hall of Virtues (so-called from the Italian frescoes on its walls) and the room where Stephen was born.
Szent István tér 1. Tel: (06 33) 415 986.
Open: Tue–Sun 9am–5pm (until 4pm in winter); www.holop.hu/~varmegom
Admission charge.

Keresztény Múzeum (Christian Museum)

This is in the Víziváros (Water Town). Its greatest treasure is the Lord's Coffin

The view from Visegrád

of Garamszentbenedek (c.1480), which was paraded in Easter processions carrying the figure of Christ crucified. *Mindszenty tér 2. Tel: (06 33) 413 880. Open: Mar–Sep, Tue–Sun 9am–5pm; Oct–Dec, Tue–Sun 11am–4pm. Admission charge.*

Visegrád

Királyi Palota (Royal Palace)

Charles Robert of Anjou put Visegrád on the map by building a palace here in 1316. Enlarged and embellished by Sigismund of Luxembourg and Matthias Corvinus in the 15th century, it was rediscovered in the 1930s. You will notice Matthias's coat of arms on the Herkules Fountain, the base of which may be seen here (the rest is in Solomon's Tower). The Lion Fountain (a replica) is so-called because sleeping lions support the five columns of the baldachino. The lion's mouth of the fountain spouted wine when the king was in festive mood.
Fő utca 23. Tel: (06) 26 398 026. Open: Tue–Sun 9am–4.30pm. Admission charge.

Salomon-torony (Solomon's Tower)

The tower was built two centuries after Salomon, son of Andrew I, was imprisoned in Visegrád, so the name is a romantic invention. It houses a museum with remnants from the royal palace.
Mátyás Király Múzeum (King Matthias Museum), tel: (06 26) 398 026. Open: May–Sep, Tue–Sun 9am–4.30pm. Admission charge.

It is well worth climbing to the Fellegvár (Citadel open daily 10am–4pm, closed in winter; *tel: (06 26) 398 101*) on the path from Nagy Lajos utca. Taxis are available in summer, and from April to September, a direct bus from Árpád híd terminus. The Hungarian crown jewels were once kept in this powerful fortress on a 350-m high peak. The views over the river and of the Börszöny Mountains are superb.

Visegrád is 40km from Budapest and reached by hourly buses from Árpád híd (Pest side), or via Road 11 by car. Twice daily, boats run from Vigadó tér in summer.

Esztergom – birthplace of King Stephen

KECSKEMÉT AND THE ALFÖLD (HUNGARIAN PLAIN)

Kecskemét

Kecskemét flourished as part of the Sultan's personal possessions during the Turkish occupation. In the 19th century it was fortunate when its vines were the only ones in Hungary to escape the phylloxera plague, and the town's wealth is reflected in its ambitious architecture and thriving cultural scene. The birthplace of the composer Zoltán Kodály and the father of Hungarian drama József Katona, it is also the production centre of the celebrated *barackpálinka* (apricot schnapps).

The main sights are clustered around the three central squares (Szabadság, Kossuth Lajos, and Katona József terek). Where Rákóczi út enters Szabadság tér, on the left is Géza Márkus's Cifra-palota (Ornate Palace, 1902), a dazzling Jugendstil building. Opposite it is the Moorish-looking former synagogue (1862), converted in 1966 into a 'House of Science and Culture'. The Town Hall, designed by Ödön Lechner and Gyula Pártos should not be missed (open: Mon–Fri 10–11am; admission charge). Its carillon of 37 bells plays at 12.05pm, 6.05pm, and 8.05pm.

Kecskemét is 85km south of Budapest and reachable by train (from Nyugati pályaudvar) and bus (from Népliget terminal). By car take M5 and the motorway (toll road) or the old Road 5.

The Alföld

Commonly referred to as the *puszta* ('abandoned'), the once forested Great Plain was heavily depopulated under the Turks and during the 18th century.

Regulation of the River Tisza in the 19th century deprived the land of its yearly alluvial deposits and turned it into the alkaline pasture that covers most of the region today.

Puszta traditions may be savoured at **Lajosmizse** and **Bugac** (both close to Kecskemét), where the *csikósok*

Budapest Excursions

UKRAINE

ROMANIA

YUGOSLAVIA

0 20 40 60 80 100 km

(cowboys) give displays of horsemanship. At Bugac there is a Puszta Museum (*www.knp.hu*) and a famous country inn (*csárda*). You may also see the grey steppe cattle and the woolly *racka* sheep.

At Lajosmizse there is a Farmhouse Museum (Tanyamuzeum).

Open: Tue–Sun 10am–5pm (until 4pm in winter). Closed: Dec & Jan).

Lajosmizse is north of Kecskemét on the old Road 5. Shows 12.30pm daily in summer. **Bugac** is to the south – turn left at Kiskúnfélegyháza. PROGRAM CENTRUM (*tel: (06 1) 317 7767; fax: (06 1) 317 9746*) and CITYRAMA (*tel: (06 1) 302 4382*).

Pécs

The attractive city of Pécs was founded by the Celts, and subsequently (as Sopianae) became the capital of the Roman province of Pannonia Valeria. King Stephen established a bishopric here in 1009. Under the Turkish occupation, Pécs was a centre of Islamic culture, boasting five *madrassas* (seminaries) and 17 mosques. In the 18th century, viticulture thrived and coal deposits were discovered, then in the 19th century the city boomed as a result of leather-making and other industries. Uranium deposits were discovered close by in the 1950s.

The Cathedral

The huge Neo-Romanesque cathedral above Szent István tér was given its

The Cathedral at Pécs

present form by the Viennese architect, Friedrich Schmidt, between 1882 and 1891, but there are 11th-, 12th-, and 14th-century remnants. Inside are 19th-century frescoes by Bertalan Székely, Károly Lotz, and others. In the Corpus Christi Chapel look for the Pastoforium of Bishop Szatmáry, a lovely Renaissance altar (1521) in red marble.

Roman Remains

Pécs has some of the earliest Christian sanctuaries in Hungary. The Roman tombs at Apáca utca 9 and the remains of the *cella trichora* (clover-leaf chapel) on the opposite side of the street are not always accessible; but the mausoleum (AD 350), just to the north on Szent István tér, is open. It contains frescoes of the Fall and Daniel in the Lion's Den.

Turkish Remains

Hungary's best preserved Turkish monuments are at Pécs. The most impressive is the Mosque of Gazi Kasim Pasha, built in 1579, using the stones of

Remains of the early Christian church in Pécs

n earlier Christian church. To the west
f the town centre is the Mosque of
kovali Hassan Pasha with a finely
arved minbar (pulpit). At Nyár utca 8,
lso to the west is a *türbe* (sepulchral
napel, 1591). Nearby is the only
urviving Turkish fountain.

ther Sights
he Bishop's Palace, on Dóm tér is
onted by a modern statue of Franz
iszt. From the other side of the square
ou enter Káptalan utca through an
rchway. The street contains no less than
ve museums, of which the Zsolnay
luseum (ceramics) is the most
teresting. The others are devoted to
dividual artists, except one, featuring
Oth-century Hungarian art. Walk along
ossuth Lajos utca to see the restored
igendstil Hotel Palatinus and the Neo-
ococo theatre, home to Péc's Ballet. In
kai utca is a splendid Zsolnay well,
hose lion's-head spout is copied from
te so-called 'Treasure of Attila'
iscovered in Romania (now in Vienna).
he works of Tivadar Csontváry Kosztka
853–1919), in the Csontváry Museum,
express a mystical vision of self
and nation. Don't miss his great
Baalbeck canvas and the poignant
Lonely Cedar.

Pécs is 180km south of Budapest.
See www.pecs.hu
Trains run direct from Budapest's Déli or
Keleti pályaudvar. Buses leave from the
terminal by the Népliget metro.

Csontváry Museum
Janus Pannonius utca 11–13. *Tel: (06 72)*
310 544. Open: Tue–Sun 10am–6pm.
Mausoleum
Szent István tér. *Tel: (06 72) 312 719.*
Open: Apr–Oct 10am–6pm; Nov–Mar
10am–4pm.
Mosque of Gazi Kasim Pasha
Széchenyi tér, now a Catholic church.
Open: summer, Mon–Sat 10am–4pm, Sun
11.30am–4pm; winter, Mon–Sat
11am–noon, Sun 11.30am–2pm.
Mosque of Jakovali Hassan Pasha
Rákóczi út 2. Open: Apr–Sep 10am–6pm.
Türbe of Idris Baba
Nyár utca 8. Closed to visitors.
Zsolnay Museum
Káptalan utca 2. *Tel: (06 72) 324 822.*
Open: Tue–Sun 10am–6pm.
Admission charge to all sights.

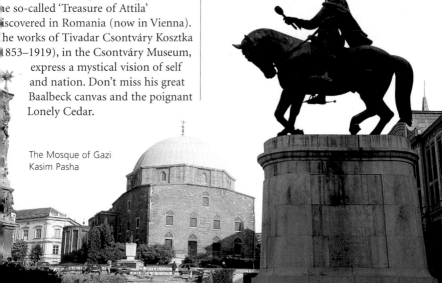

The Mosque of Gazi
Kasim Pasha

View from the main square

Szentendre

Szentendre (St Andrew) has a Balkan charm rarely encountered in Hungary. It was founded as a town for Serbian refugees after the catastrophic defeat of Serbia by the Turks at Kosovo in 1389. A second wave of immigrants came in 1690, fleeing the wrath of the Turks after an abortive uprising. Both the earlier Hungarian kings and the Habsburgs favoured these refugees from the south. The settlers were able to exploit their trading privileges and the town's proximity to the Danube to become wealthy. Several Orthodox churches were built here in the 18th century, usually on the site of wooden predecessors, each representing a community drawn from a common provenance in the Slav homeland.

The Serb population has dwindled in the 20th century and now only about 100 are left out of Szentendre's 20,000 inhabitants. Some of the churches have been sold and are difficult to access.

Szentendre's other claim to fame is the artists' colony started here in the early years of the 20th century, and still going strong.

Belgrád Székesegyház Church (Belgrade Cathedral)

The episcopal church is open only at times of mass (Sun 10am, 4pm, Sat 5pm in winter, 6pm in summer). The iconostasis (1777), the bishop's throne, and the pulpit are notable. Do not miss the nearby Szerb Egyházművészeti Gyűjtemény (Collection of Ecclesiastical Treasures) which contains fine icons and other works by Orthodox masters.
Pátriárka utca 5. Tel: (06 26) 312 399. Open: Mar–Sep, Tue–Sun 10am–6pm; Oct–Dec, Tue–Sun 10am–4pm; Jan & Feb, Fri–Sun 10am–4pm. Admission charge.

Blagoveštenska Church (Church of the Annunciation)

Commissioned by Greek merchants and built by Andreas Mayerhoffer (1754), this church has a fine iconostasis (1804) by a Serb artist from Buda.
Edge of Fő tér. Open: most days 9am–5pm. Admission charge.

Plébániatemplom (Parish Church of St John)

Steps lead up from Fő tér to Templom tér, on which stands the church of the Catholic Dalmatian community. You can only view it from the porch, but it is worth the climb for the marvellous panorama of the town from the square.

Pozarevacka Church (Church of St Michael the Archangel)

The church was built in 1763 on the site of a wooden predecessor. Here and in the Blagoveštenska an atmospheric tape of Orthodox chant is played for the benefit of visitors.

Kossuth Lajos utca. Open: in summer, Fri–Sun 11am–5pm. Admission charge.

Ferenczy Museum

The museum is devoted to artistic works by the Ferenczy family, of whom the father, Károly (1862–1917), was the leading figure in the Nagybánya artists' colony.

Fő tér 6. Tel: (06 26) 310 244. Open: 16 Mar–31 Oct 10am–5.30pm; 1 Nov–15 Mar, Fri–Sun 10am–4pm. Closed: Mon. Admission charge.

Margit Kovács Museum

Billed as Hungary's leading ceramicist, Margit Kovács (1902–77) made sculpture and reliefs that drew eclectically on the traditions of folk art and fine art. The claims made for her work have been recklessly inflated.

Vastagh György utca 1. Tel: (06) 263 10244. Open: 16 Mar–31 Oct 10am–6pm; 1 Nov–15 Mar 10am–4pm. Closed: Mon (open daily during summer tourist season). Admission charge.

Szabadtéri Néprajzi Múzeum (Village Museum or Skanzen)

Known as a *skanzen* after a pioneering Swedish ethnographical reconstruction of village life and architecture, the museum will eventually show typical peasant dwellings, churches, and functional agricultural buildings from 10 regions of Hungary. At weekends there are often demonstrations of crafts and folklore programmes.

4km west of Szentendre on Szabadságforrás út. Tel: (06 26) 312 304/502 500; www.sznm.hu Open: Apr–Oct, Tue–Sun 9am–5pm. Hourly buses from HÉV station.

Service in an Orthodox church

Marcipán Múzeum
(Marzipan Museum)
Dumtsa Jenő utca 12, entrance through
the cake shop. Tel: (06 26) 311 931;
www.szabomarcipan.hu Open: daily
10am–6pm.

Városi Tömegközlekedési Múzeum
(Museum of the Hungarian City Public
Transport)
Very interesting for tram fans.
Dózsa György út. Tel: (06 26) 314 280;
www.bkv.hu/muzeum/szentendre.html.
Open: Apr–Oct, Tue–Sun 10am–5pm.

Szentendre is 23km northwest of Budapest.
There is a direct rail link (HÉV) from
Batthyány tér and hourly buses from
Árpád híd bus terminus. In summer boats
leave from Vigadó tér twice daily.

Vác
Mentioned by Ptolemy in his
Geographia, the ancient town of Vác
was made an episcopal see by King
Stephen. The town was rich – the Vác
silver mark was the main local currency
of the 14th century – and the bishops
were powerful. One of them, Kristóf
Migazzi, had the Triumphal Arch near
Március 15 tér erected for Maria
Theresa's visit in 1764. Its architect,
Isidore Canevale, built the imposing
Neo-Classical cathedral on Konstantin
tér in 1777. It contains a fine fresco (*The
Trinity* by Franz Anton Maulbertsch) in
its cupola.
    Worth seeing also are the finds of the
crypt of the Dominican church.
34km north of Budapest. Trains from
Nyugati pályaudvar. Szentendre and Vác
can be seen in one day. Buses run hourly

from Szentendre to Váci Rév where a ferry
meets the bus and takes you to the centre
of Vác, from where buses return at regular
intervals till 10.30pm.

Vácrátót
This fascinating botanical garden
comprises 12,000 species of plants and
trees, artificial lakes, follies, and a
watermill.
25km north of Budapest. Infrequent trains
from Nyugati pályaudvar. By car, take
Road 2 to Szödliget and turn right.
Alkotmány utca 2/4, tel: (06 28) 369 398.
Open: Apr–Oct 8am–6pm; Nov–Mar
until 4pm. Admission charge.

Zebegény
Károly Kós's vernacular church is the
main sight in this artists' haunt beside
the Danube. The stylised frescoes
(*Emperor Constantine's Vision of the
Cross, Saint Helena Discovering the True
Cross*) are by the Gödöllő artist, Aladár
Körösfői-Kriesch (*see p83*).
50km north of Budapest. Roads 2 & 12
via Vác; very slow boats from Vigadó tér
in summer; the Szob or Sturovo bound
trains via Vác from Nyugati pályaudvar.

Gödöllő
This Baroque mansion is also called the
Sissy Mansion after Elizabeth (popularly
known as Sissy), wife of the Austro-
Hungarian emperor Franz Josef I (*see
p8*) who loved coming here. After 1945
it became a home for aged people and
later, a Soviet military barracks.
Take the HÉV from Örs Vezér tere until
the Szabadság tér stop. The palace is right
across the street. Tel: (06 28) 410 124;
www.kiralyikastely.hu Open: Tue–Sun

10am–6pm (5pm in winter), last tour at 5pm. Closed: Jan.

Zsámbék

The ruined Romanesque and late Gothic church here was built for the Premonstratensians in the 13th century and later taken over by the Paulites. Another attraction here is the Lamp Museum, housed in a typical Swabian cottage (the village was Swabian until the expulsion of many Germans following World War II).

33km west of Budapest. Buses from Széna tér (next to Moszkva tér). Lamp Museum: Magyar utca 18. Tel: (06 23) 342 212. Open: daily 8am–6pm. Admission charge.

The village of Zsámbék

Getting Away From It All

'Budapest and the Danube present one of the most beautiful river-town landscapes anywhere: perhaps the most beautiful in Europe, on a par with London and the Thames or Paris and the Seine.'

JULES ROMAINS

1926

Waxworks in the Castle Hill caves

BUDA CAVES

A number of exciting caves have been discovered in the Buda Hills, and four of them can be visited without difficulty. Comprising ancient and long inactive vents for hot springs, the caves have been formed along tectonic fractures.

Rock Chapel in the caves in Gellért Hill

Castle Hill Caves

The interior of Castle Hill is honeycombed with caves which were structurally improved by the inhabitants over the years. Remnants of Palaeolithic culture have been found here. The 10km of passages and chambers were used in World War II as an air-raid shelter and field hospital. A gruesome waxworks exhibition (Budavári Panoptikum) illustrating the bloodiest scenes of Hungarian history now occupies a part of them.

Úri utca 9. Tel: (06 1) 489 3280.
Open: daily 9.30am–7.30pm.
Admission charge. Bus: 16, or várbusz to Dísz tér.

Gellért-hegy Cave (Rock Chapel)

The earliest human habitation of the region was probably in the Gellért caves. A chapel consecrated here in 1926 was walled up by the Communists but reopened in 1990.

Szent Gellért rakpart 1. Open: 9am–9pm.
Trams: 18, 19, 47 & 49. Bus: 86 to Szent Gellért tér.

Pálvölgyi Barlang

This 7-km long cave came to light in

902 when the son of the local quarry manager squeezed himself through a gap in the rocks. The highlight of the tour is the 'zoo', so-called because the drip formations recall elephants and crocodiles.

zépvölgyi út 162. Tel: (01) 325 9505.
Open: Apr–Oct, Tue–Sat 10am–4pm.
Admission charge. Bus: 65 (five stops)
from Kolosy tér, Óbuda.

Szemlőhegyi Barlang

This is renowned for its 'peastone' formations, like bunches of grapes with little stalactites suspended from them. Part of the cave is used for treating people with respiratory diseases. There is a small exhibition about local speleology in the reception building.

Pusztaszeri út 35. Tel: (01) 325 6001.
Open: Wed–Fri 10am–3pm, Sat & Sun
10am–4pm. Admission charge. Bus: 29
(four stops) from Kolosy tér, Óbuda.

BUDAI-HEGYSÉG (THE BUDA HILLS)

The easiest way of seeing the Buda Hills is to make a tour with the cogwheel railway and the Children's (formerly 'Pioneer') Railway (*see p154*).

The cogwheel railway (Fogaskerekű Vasút) ascends from Városmajor along wooded slopes past the Svábhegy (a Swabian village founded under Maria Theresa), and the Pető Institute for helping brain-damaged children, to Regec on Széchenyi-hegy. Nearby is the end-station for the Children's Railway (Gyermekvasút), staffed by children under the supervision of adults. You can take it to the terminus at Hűvösvölgy, or get off at Normafa (first stop), or János-hegy (fourth stop) for rambles with convenient return connections. From Normafa, a 2-km walk (bear left) brings you to the **Budakeszi Game Park**, with return buses to Moszkva tér. From János-hegy (529m, lookout tower), a chairlift descends to Zugligeti út (bus 158 to Moszkva tér).

For the cogwheel railway take trams 18 & 56 from Moszkva tér along Szilágyi Erzsébet fasor to the stop opposite the Hotel Budapest (second stop). The Children's Railway runs every 45–60 minutes 9am–6.30pm in summer, 9am–5pm in winter. Budapest local tickets and passes, but not the Budapest Card, are valid on the Children's Railway. Budakeszi Game Park open: daily 9am–5pm (direct connection with bus 22 from Moszkva tér to Korányi Sanatorium). The János-hegy chairlift operates 9am–5pm or 9.30am–4pm according to season.

> At the ticket offices for the Pálvölgyi and Szemlőhegyi caves you can apply to join special tours of several other caves not normally open to the public. Appropriate dress will be provided. It is essential that you are fit and in sound health.

Aboard the Children's Railway

Danube Islands

Of the islands on the Budapest stretch of the Danube, the small Óbuda Island is largely of historical interest: a shipyard was founded here in 1836 on the initiative of Count Széchenyi, and worked until the 1990s. At the north end are the ruins of the Roman governor's palace. Margaret Island is the city's loveliest park (*see p58 for details, and pp44–5 for a walk around it*). Csepel Island begins in Budapest and extends to the Great Hungarian Plain.

Window boxes in bloom
the Wekerle settlement

CSEPEL SZIGET (CSEPEL ISLAND)

This elongated sliver of land begins as Budapest's industrialised 21st District and ends 54km to the south. The origins of the district's heavy industry go back to 1882 when Manfred Weiss founded a factory producing ration tins for troops of the Austro-Hungarian army. He moved to Csepel in 1890 and expanded into armaments. The Communists nationalised the business after the war, and the workers of 'Red Csepel' were supposed to be a bulwark of proletarian solidarity (they even had the dubious pleasure of being represented by the Stalinist dictator Rákosi). Nevertheless, they were the last to hold out against Russian tanks in the 1956 revolution.

Csepel's industry is now largely obsolete and it is planned to use some of its vacant lots for exhibitions and the like. Across the Danube on the Buda side can be seen the restored Baroque **Nagytétényi Castle** which has a good display of the history of European furniture (*tel: (06 1) 207 5462; open: Tue–Sun, Mar–Oct 10am–6pm; Nov–Feb 10am–4pm; bus: 3 from Móricz Zsigmond körtér, from Csepel, bus 138 to Campona shopping mall, and then bus 3*).

Ráckeve

The place most worth visiting on Csepel Island lies to the south, where the ugly industrial suburbs

PRINCE EUGENE OF SAVOY

The greatest general in the history of Central Europe, Prince Eugene was responsible for clearing Hungary of the Turks after participating in the reconquest of Buda (1686). The Battle of Zenta (1697) was decisive in removing the Ottoman menace once and for all. Eugene was no less successful when allied with the Duke of Marlborough against the French in the War of the Spanish Succession (1701–14). His statue stands before the National Gallery on Castle Hill.

give way to cottages and gardens. Rác means Serb in Hungarian, and the small town was originally populated by Serbs from Keve, who fled here in the 15th century. Today, of Ráckeve's 8,500 inhabitants, only a handful are Serb.

Szerb Templom (Serbian Church)
Ráckeve's church survives and is well worth a visit. The main Gothic structure dates to 1487, but the two side-chapels were added later, together with a Baroque spire. Inside are colourful frescoes (1771) in Byzantine style by Tódor

Gruntovic (who was apparently an Albanian from Kosovo). The sequence begins to the right of the entrance with the Nativity and continues round the church walls, ending with the Resurrection. The Baroque iconostasis (1768) is also striking.
Viola utca 1. Tel: (06 24) 385 985. Open: Tue–Sat 10am–noon, 2–5pm, Sun 2–5pm.

**Savoyai Kastély
(Mansion of Prince Eugene of Savoy)**
The land on which this delightfully elegant mansion was built originally

Detail of a chateau façade at Ráckeve

Prince Eugene of Savoy's elegant mansion at Ráckeve

belonged to the Habsburgs and was sold by them to Prince Eugene after the Turkish wars. He employed Johann Lukas von Hildebrandt (later to build the magnificent Belvedere Palace in Vienna for him) to construct a Baroque Schloss between 1702 and 1722. The Neo-Classical dome was added in the 19th century. The splendid interiors have unfortunately been destroyed and the mansion is now a smart hotel. *Kossuth-Lajos utca 95. Hotel. Tel: (06 24) 485 253; www.elender.hu/~savoyai*

Ráckeve is 46km south of Budapest. The HÉV suburban train leaves Közvágóhíd terminus in Pest and takes 75 minutes. Trams 2 & 24 end at Közvágóhíd.

Wekerle-Telep (Wekerle Settlement)

In the 19th District (Kispest) a remarkable experiment in 20th-century social housing reflects the ambitious plans for city expansion developed by Budapest's mayor, István Bárczy.

Inspired by the principles of the English garden suburb, the Wekerle Housing Estate was built over 20 years from 1909 as a completely self-contained village for employees of the municipality. It consists of 650 single-storey villas and 270 bungalows, and bears the name of Sándor Wekerle, the far-sighted and liberal prime minister between 1892 and 1895, and again between 1906 and 1910.

Wekerle reformed the Hungarian

rrency and successfully fought to limit erical influence in matters of the state. he principal architect for the estate was e polymath Károly Kós (*see box*), who vested the wooden, gabled, and lconied houses with a Transylvanian arm (albeit pseudo). Four ornamental tes stand at the entrances to the ntral Kós Károly tér. The west gate is rticularly interesting, consisting of a ge planked gable rising over sticated plinths. Another gate mixes rnacular decoration with Renaissance atures.

The houses have their own vegetable rdens – a rarity within the city – and e different quarters are divided by afy avenues and squares.

Metro (blue line) to Határ út; then bus 194 to Kós Károly tér, or buses 99 & 99A from Blaha Lujza tér metro, Népsúnholz utca, via Hatar út metro to Kós Kárdy tér.

Károly Kós (1883–1977)

Born in Temesvár (now Romanian Timisoara) in Transylvania, Kós won major commissions in Budapest when still in his twenties. As an architect he was influenced by Finnish architecture and the English Arts and Crafts movement. He was also a gifted writer, illustrating and printing his own works. In Budapest, in addition to the Wekerle Settlement, he designed the buildings for the zoo in 'national romantic style'; dwelling houses that recall the work of Arts and Crafts architect, Charles Voysey, in England; and schools and churches in the vernacular style.

Icomies and gabled houses in the Wekerle Settlement

Hungary's folk traditions have long reflected diverse ethnic groups (Ruthenians, Slavonians, Slovaks, Rumanians and Serbs, as well as Magyars). Despite commercialisation, beautiful handicrafts are still produced, and the charm of folk song and dance undimmed. Surviving peasant homes provide a fascinating insight into a way of life not totally extinct.

Folk art shops are found at all popular tourist spots. Visitors to Budapest may first glimpse folk embroidery as they pass the Transylvanian women who sell their wares at the entrance to the metro or on Castle Hill. Their speciality is the lovely red (or sometimes blue) 'tulip' or 'heart' pattern on a white background. Other regions produce delicate open work, wool embroidered cushion ends, and beautifully ornamented aprons, tablecloths, or handkerchiefs. Dense, multi-coloured needlework for folk costumes is a Matyó speciality from northern Hungary.

walls and roofs thatched with reeds.

Folk entertainment – dancing, singing, and seasonal celebrations – may be seen all over Hungary, but especially at Hollókő in the north, home of the Palóc people. Easter time here harks back to pagan purification and fertility rites. The girls paint beautiful floral designs on eggs, and must run the gauntlet of young men sprinkling them with well water.

ttery is a traditional wedding gift. om the Great Plain come water jars th an ochre glaze and attractive loured pitchers, or plates with flower, d, or star patterns. Look out, too, for e smoky black pottery of Nádudvar in e Hajdúság region.

The horsemen, shepherds, and vineherds of the Great Plain specialise carved artefacts, such as whip ndles, crooks, axes, mirror frames, or bacco boxes. Look out for beautiful lk carving if you visit the Protestant urches of Southern Transdanubia and e Upper Tisza.

The place to see rural architecture is *skanzen* (an open-air museum village ch as the one at Szentendre, *see p131*). e houses often had wattle-and-daub

Hungarian folk culture includes music, dancing, pottery, and textiles

colourful brochure of folklore events and erformances is obtainable from Tourinform, ütő utca 2, or Vörösmarty tér, Vigadó tca 6. *Tel: (06 80) 66 0044 (toll free)* or 38 8080. (*Also see* Shopping *p143*.)

Shopping

In the celebrated Váci utca in the heart of Pest (*see p104*) you will find long-established shops selling folk art and books alongside newcomers like Adidas. Souvenir-hunters will find plenty to interest them on Castle Hill, while the Fortuna Passage opposite the Hilton has a good bookshop and antiques. Other items to look out for are Herend porcelain and Zsolnay faience. Food delicacies include salami, goose liver, and Tokaji wine.

Antiques can be very good value

Card use and acceptance is increasing. Most big shops, and petrol stations, accept VISA, VISA Electron Eurocard/MasterCard and Maestro cards. American Express and Diners Club are less used by Hungarians.

Antiques

The state-owned chain **Bizományi Áruház Vállalat (BÁV)** is best for antiques and furniture.
Szent István körút 3.
Tel: (06 1) 473 0666.
Ferenciek tere 12.
Tel: (06 1) 318 3381.
Párizsi utca 2. Tel: (06 1) 318 6217. Branches near Ferenciek tere.
Detre-Ferenczi
Váci utca 51.
Tel: (06 1) 317 7743.
Patina
Váci utca 46.
Tel: (06 1) 337 9627.

Régiség-Vári Antikvitás
Szentháromság utca 7 (Castle Hill).
Tel: (06 1) 212 3715.

Art Galleries
BÁV Galéria
Falk Miksa utca 32.
Tel: (06 1) 353 1975.
Dorottya Galéria
Dorottya utca 8.
Tel: (06 1) 266 0877.
Kortárs Galéria
Váci utca 25.
Tel: (06 1) 266 3127.

Books and Maps
There are many secondhand bookshops on the Múzeum körút between Astoria and Kálvin tér metro stations opposite the Hungarian National Museum. Other good shops to visit are:
Cartographia
The largest selection of up-to-date local and

foreign maps is available here.
Bajcsy-Zsilinszky út 37.
Tel: (06 1) 312 6001.
Központi Antikvárium
Old prints; also second-hand books.
Múzeum körút 13–15.
Tel: (06 1) 317 3781.

Children's Wear
Bambini
Margit Körút 56. Anker köz 1. Villányi út 42.
Brendon
Váci út 168.
Tel: (06 1) 329 9704.

Delicatessens
La Boutique des Vins
The owner is chef of the Gundel Restaurant.
József Attila utca 12.
Tel: (06 1) 317 5919.
PICK
The house of the famou Hungarian salami. The restaurant upstairs serve

quick, economical
lunches on weekdays.
Near the Parliament,
Kossuth Lajos tér 9.
Tel: (06 1) 331 7783.

Department Stores
Corvin
Blaha Lujza tér 1.
Tel: (06 1) 266 7788.
Luxus
Vörösmarty tér 3.
Tel: (06 1) 318 2277.
Skála Metro
opp railway station,
Nyugati tér1–2.
Tel: (06 1) 353 0500.
Skála Budapest
Október 23, utca 6–10.
Tel: (06 1) 385 0850.

Folk Art
Embroidery, lace, faience,
wax figures, and painted
Easter eggs. Shops on the
Váci utca and Castle Hill.
Folk-Art Rt
Régiposta utca 12.
Tel: (01) 266 5334.
Lux Folklor
Váci utca 6.
Tel: (01) 318 6980.
Népművészeti bolt/
Folk-Art Rt
Rákóczi út 32.
Tel: (01) 342 0753.

Foreign Language
Bookshops
Bestsellers
English and American
books and newspapers

V Október 6 utca 11.
Tel: (01) 312 1295.
Libri Studium
Váci utca 22.
Tel: (06 1) 318 5680.
Litea Bookshop and Tea-
Garden
Hess András tér 4
(Fortuna Passage).
Tel: (06 1) 375 6987.
Párizsi Udvar
Idegennyelvű
Könyvesbolt
Petőfi Sándor utca 2.
Tel: (06 1) 235 0380.

Jewellery
Richter Károly
Országház utca 12, (Castle
Hill). Tel: (01) 356 1746.

Music
FOTEX Records
Szervita tér 2.
Tel: (06 1) 318 3395.
MCD
Classical and pop music
from Hungary.
Vörösmarty tér 1.
Rózsavölgyi Zeneműbolt
Szervita tér 5.
Tel: (06 1) 318 3500.

Shoes
Vass Handmade Shoes
Ltd
Haris köz 2.
Tel: (06 1) 318 2375.

MALLS
Budapest now also has
numerous new shopping

centres (malls). The first
of these, Polus and Duna
Plaza, opened in 1996
and served as a tangible
sign of 'Westernisation'.
Every mall has a super-
market and restaurants as
well as clean, free toilets.
  Malls shops also offer
longer opening hours
(10am–8pm, Mon–Sat,
and till 6pm on Sun).
Almost every part of
town has its own malls.
Campona
Has a tropicarium, an
oceanarium, and indoor
rainforest in addition to
al the usual attractions.
Nagytétényi út 37–45.
Tel: (06 1) 424 3000.
Duna Plaza
Váci út 178.
Tel:(06 1) 465 1666.
Europark
For serious shoppers!
Üllői út 201.
Tel: (06 1) 347 1607.
Mammut I and II
Houses Hungary's largest
bookstore, a multiplex
cinema, bowling alley and
300 shops.
Széna tér.
Tel: (06 1) 345 8020.
Westend City Center
Budapest largest with 400
shops, a waterfall, roof
garden, and multiplex
cinema.
Váci út 1–3.
Tel: (06 1) 238 7777.

MARKETS
Flea Markets

The legendary flea markets (*bolhapiac*) of Budapest, though not for the faint-hearted, are a paradise for junk fanatics. Since the collapse of Communism the amount of Marxist-Leninist bric-à-brac to be found in them has increased; there are even Russian army uniforms and caps, sold off by impoverished Soviet troops before their departure.

Ecseri Piac (Ecseri Flea Market)

This was officially renamed Használtcikk (used items) market after one of its several moves from its original location on Ecseri út, but everyone uses the old name. The outer stalls (*kirakodó*) are loaded with knicknacks – most of it uninspiring, the good stuff having been sold to dealers in the early hours. These dealers (many of them Slavs or gypsies) occupy booths in the centre, and it is here that you might find bargains. Much of their stock comes from peasants, persuaded to part with their family heirlooms when the dealers canvassed a village.

The most interesting goods at Ecseri are decorative silver and Russian icons. Unfortunately, the silver is usually being sold illegally (under Hungarian law a permit is required to deal in it), while the icons may well have been looted from Ukrainian churches. Not long ago the police confiscated some icons that had been stolen from somewhere near Chernobyl – on the grounds that they were contaminated with radiation, not because they were stolen! Other items of interest said to crop up include 'bentwood' chairs made by the Viennese Thonet company, old radios, and copper lamps. It is best to go to Ecseri with a Hungarian who knows the ropes and you should beware of pickpockets.

Vegetables on display

*Nagykőrösi út 156 in the 19th District.
Open: Mon–Fri 8am–4pm, Sat
8am–3pm. Bus: 54 from Boráros tér, or
bus 154 Mon to Fri from Határ út metro
station.*

Józsefvárosi Piac
(Market in the Józsefváros)
The self-styled 'Worldwide Business
Centre' is really a Third World souk.
Traders come from as far afield as China
and Vietnam, but chiefly from the
former Soviet Union, Bulgaria, and
Romania. They trade cheap goods for
things not available back home.
American kitsch is big here, as is liquor
of uncertain provenance, used car parts,
cigarette lighters – anything, in short,
that might have fallen off the back of a
lorry or turned up in the attic.
*Kőbányai út 9 (10th District).
Open: daily till 1pm. Tram: 28 from
Blaha Lujza tér, or bus 9 from Deák
Ferenc tér.*

Another interesting flea market is held
outside the **Petőfi Hall** (Petőfi Csarnok)
in the Városliget.
*Open: Sat & Sun 7am–2pm. Metro: to
Széchenyi fürdö, or trolley buses 70, 72
& 74.*

Food and General Markets
Központi Vásárcsarnok
(Central Market)
This is a fabulous 19th-century covered
market. It was one of five opened in the
1890s (*see p31*) and is a protected
monument. There are over 100 stalls on
two floors selling meat, vegetables, fruit,
and even flower seeds and pottery; note
that most stalls close around noon.

Local flea market

*Vámház körút 1–3. Tel: (01) 217 6865.
Open: Mon–Thu 6am–4pm, Fri
6am–7pm, Sat 6am–3pm. Trams: 47 &
49 to Fővám tér.*

Rákóczi Téri Csarnok
(Market Hall on Rákóczi Tér)
Another market hall from the 1890s.
Rákóczi tér 7–8. Tel (06 1) 210 2565.

Lehel Piac (Lehel Market)
Futuristic new market hall opened in
2002 in an old market location.
Metro: Lehel tér

Western supermarkets have moved in
on Budapest – including Spar and
Tesco. Every shopping mall also has a
supermarket, usually a Spar or Match.

Entertainment

Ballet performances are well attended

Ballet

Ballet is not a major feature of the Budapest scene, but performances by prima ballerinas Katalin Volf and Ildikó Pongor are worth looking out for. The *corps de ballet* is resident at the State Opera. Foreign companies make guest appearances at Budapest arts festivals (*see p149*). Ballets and musicals are usually staged in the Thália Theatre (Thália Szihaz), Nagymezö utca 22–24, *tel: (06 1) 312 4230.*

Cinema

The cinematic tradition is strong in Hungary and there are currently over 20 cinemas in Budapest. Works of the giants of the Hungarian film scene – directors such as Miklós Jancsó, Pál Sándor, or István Szabó – will be well known to Western film buffs. Although the big co-productions such as *Colonel Redl* or *Mephisto* have been widely exposed abroad, the occasional Budapest summer season of home-grown movies affords a chance to see more obscure works with English subtitles. *Pesti Müsor*

is the best source for information on such events – look under *A budapesti mozik müsora* (you'll need a friend on hand to translate). *Pest Est,* a cinema programme (*www.pestiest.hu*), is available free at cinemas, bars, and restaurants, though it is in Hungarian.

Films in English, German, French, and Italian

With the lifting of censorship in 1989, a tidal wave of American products – sex 'n' violence to the fore – engulfed the Budapest movie screens. Now things have settled down, you can see most recent mainstream films with the original soundtrack. The best sources of information are the detailed movie programmes in *Budapest Week* (*www.budapestweek.hu*) and *The Budapest Sun* (*www.budapestsun.hu*). Classics are shown at the Örökmozgo Filmmúzeum (*tel: (06 1) 342 2167*). There are usually some seven or eight films in the repertory at any given time.

Opera

Opera is popular in Hungary and has a distinguished tradition going back to the opening of Miklós Ybl's opera house in 1882 (*see p81*). New productions are staged during the spring music festival and the autumn/winter season.

If you want specifically to see Hungarian opera, look out for Béla Bartók's *Kékszakállú herceg vára* (Bluebeard's Castle), Ferenc Erkel's *Bán Bán*, Károly Goldmark's *Sába királynöje* (The Queen of Sheba), and Zoltán Kódaly's *Háry János*.

The State Opera went through a bad patch in the last phase of Communism because of incompetent management; the main problem today is lack of money. However, leading expatriate singers (Sylvia Sass or Éva Marton, for instance) sometimes visit, and the modest price of a ticket is well worth it.

Opera Venues
Magyar Állami Operaház (State Opera House)
Andrássy út 22. Tel: (06 1) 353 0170.
Box office at Andrássy út 20.
Tel: (06 1) 332 7914; www.opera hu
Erkel Színház (Erkel Theatre)
Köztársaság tér 30. Tel: (01) 333 0540.

Operetta and Musicals
The heyday of operetta (*see p86*) followed the formation of the Austro-Hungarian Empire in 1867 and lasted until the end of World War I. It has been largely superseded by the musical, of which two popular Hungarian examples are the rock-operas *István, a király (Stephen the King)* and *Attila* (first produced in 1993).

Operetta Venues
Fővárosi Operett Színház (Operetta Theatre)
Nagymezo utca 17. Tel: (06 1) 353 2172.
Pesti Vigadó (The Pest Redoute)
From May to October, on Tuesday, Thursday and Saturday, the theatre offers a programme of hits from Lehár, Strauss, Kálmán, Ábrahám, and others.
Vigadó tér 2. Tel: (06 1) 1318 9167; www.vigadó.hu

Theatre
The obvious problem about visiting the theatre in Budapest is the language barrier. **Katona József Theatre** (Petőfi Sándor utca 6, *tel: (06 1) 318 6599*) provides English language summaries of plays on request. **Merlin Theatre** (Gerlóczy utca 4, *tel: (06 1) 117 9338*) is currently the only venue for English-language productions, but these are few and far between. The latest on the city entertainment scence is the new Hungarian National Theatre (Namzeti Színház), located between the Danube and Soroksári út, which opened in March 2002.

The Operetta Theatre

MUSIC

In Hungary the classical tradition, nutured by the Music Academy (*see pp82–3 & p85*), is very strong. Names such as Széll, Solti, Doráti, and Ormándy are familiar to all music lovers.

The new generation includes outstanding soloists such as Dezsö Ránki and Zoltán Kocsis (piano), Vilmos Szabadi (violin), and Miklós Perényi (cello), and

At the Music Academy

distinguished composers such as Franz Liszt, Ferenc Erkel, Béla Bartók, Zoltán Kodály, Ernö Dohnány, as well as individuals such as György Ligeti and György Kurtág, who made considerable impact on the modern music scene.

Main Classical Music Venues

Budapest Kongresszusi Központ (Budapest Convention Centre)
A large modern concert hall away from the centre.
Jagelló út 1–3.
Tel: (06 1) 372 5700.
Hilton Szálló (Dominican Courtyard of the Hilton Hotel)
Chamber music concerts in summer.
Hess András tér 1–3.
Pesti Vigadó (The Pest Redoute)
(*See p82 & p147.*)
Vigadó tér 2.
Tel: (06 1) 318 9167,
www.vidago.hu
Zeneakadémia (Music Academy)
Highly recommended for acoustics and exotic architecture.
Liszt Ferenc tér 8.
Tel: (06 1) 342 0179.

Frequent organ and choral music performances are

BOOKING FOR MUSICAL PERFORMANCES

Tickets for classical music (symphony concerts, chamber music and recitals) are sold at the Központi Jegyirodá (Central Booking Office) at Andrássy út 15 (*tel: (06 1) 267 1267*). Tickets for outdoor performances in summer are sold at:
Ticket Express, Jókai utca 40 (*tel: (06 30 30 30 999, www. ticketexpress.hu*);
Music Mix (*tel: (06 1) 266 7070, www.musicmix.hu*).
Otherwise apply to the box-offices at the venues concerned.

Pesti Műsor publishes information on forthcoming musical events every Thursday under 'zene' in the English language newspapers and in brochures obtainable from Tourinform (*see p189*).

The Central Ticket Office carries the useful Koncert Kalendárium published in both Hungarian and German listing musical events a month in advance.

also held in the Matthias Church and St Stephen's Basilica.

Modern Music

If you prefer New Wave, visit TRAFO. *Liliom utca 41. Tel: (06 1) 215 1600; www.trafo.hu*

Folk Music

**Hagyományok Háza
(House of the Traditions)**
Home of the State Folk Ensemble.
Corvin tér 8. Tel: (06 1) 201 5928.

**Fövárosi Müvelödési Ház
(City Cultural House)**
Easily the best group for Hungarian folk music (Muzsikás with Márta Sebestyén) plays here on Tuesdays.
Fehérvári út 47. Tel: (06 1) 203 3868.

Festivals

The first important music month of the year is March, with the Budapest Spring Festival during its second half. The festival offers '10 days of 1,000 events in 100 venues', and many big-name musicians make guest appearances. The festival programme can be obtained from Tourinform, *tel (06 1) 486 3311,* or *www.festivalcity.hu*

Summer sees performances on the open-air stages of the city (notably opera at the Margaret Island Theatre, *tel: (06 1) 340 5540)* and at venues within striking distance of the capital (for example, at the country house at Martonvásár). Baroque operas are now being performed each summer in the courtyard of the Zichy Palace in Óbuda. There is an autumn Festival of Church Music, which provides a good chance to hear interesting works by Hungarian

Concert poster

composers past and present. In November, a choral festival titled *Vox Pacis* takes place. The number of events and mini-festivals is continually increasing with sponsorship.

For the young, a week-long Island (Sziget) Modern Music Festival (*www.sziget.hu*) on the Óbudai *sziget* in mid-summer is very popular. Daily and weekly tickets are available in advance, and, if you are early, on the spot as well. *(HÉV: from Batthyány tér metro to Fiatorigát).*

Gypsies and their Music

Gypsies first came to Hungary in the 15th century from Asia through the Balkan region, and are now the largest minority in the country (5 per cent of the population); they are also the most underprivileged. In the public mind they are associated less with music than with poverty, crime, and unemployment. Though no longer nomadic, they are still among the most deprived section of society. To combat this, a 'Roma Parliament' was recently formed, and its leaders are trying to raise national consciousness and improve the gypsies' tainted image.

Music has traditionally offered gypsies a way out of the cultural ghetto. Gypsy players accompanied conscription drives across the land in the 18th century; gypsy bands played for the nobility and the gentry in the 19th century, when they began to become figures of romance. Around the turn of the century they were romanticised in operettas like *Gypsy Life* (1904), *Gypsy Love* (1910), and the *Gypsy Bandleader* (1912). In the late 19th century, the *Neue Freie Presse* in Vienna pointed out how members of gypsy musician families had benefited from the Hungarian gypsy cult: 'They no longer tell fortunes or ply the tinker's trade, but instead put on a dinner jacket and fiddle for the *beau monde* from eleven at night till five in the morning'.

Contrary to popular belief, what the musicians play is not the true music of the gypsies. According to the composer Béla Bartók, 'They are simply performers of Hungarian popular song'; and he added: 'There is of course gypsy music – songs with texts in gypsy language. These are never played or sung by gypsies in public.'

Today the smarter restaurants in Budapest all have their own gypsy ensemble playing evergreens from Viennese operetta and the frenzied Hungarian *csárdás*. These are the aristocrats of the gypsy world, famous for their ready wit and happy-go-lucky temperament, unextinguished by centuries of persecution.

Traditional gypsy music and dance

The 'Ybl Kiosk', now a casino

NIGHTLIFE

Budapest's nightlife has thrown aside the prudery and inhibitions of the Communist era, and now offers a range of floor shows, clubs, and discos. These last tend to come and go – the ones mentioned below look to have staying power, but there is no guarantee. Most places exact an entry fee or cover charge and drinks can be quite expensive by local standards. In general, the average traveller might find the jazz locales more congenial than the rock venues; floor shows are better in the hotels.

Casinos
Las Vegas Casino
In the Hyatt Ragency Hotel.
Roosevelt tér 2.
Tel: (06 1) 317 6022.
Open: 2pm–5am.
Tropicana Casino
Vidagó utca 2.
Tel: (061) 266 3062.
Open: 2pm–5am.
Várkert Casino
Sophisticated casino in the former 'Ybl Kiosk' (Royal Castle pumphouse).
Ybl Miklós tér 9.
Tel: (01) 202 4244.
Open: 2pm–5am.

Discos
Alcatraz Club
Nyár utca 1.
Tel: (06 1) 478 6010.
Metro: Blaha Lujza tér.
Bahnhof Music Club
Teréz körút 55, behind the Nyugati Railway Station.
Tel: (06 1) 302 4751.
Buddy Holly Club
A haven of (and for) golden oldies.
Kruzspér utca 2–4.
Tel: (06 1) 209 9368.
E-Club
In the Népliget by the Planitarium.
Tel: (06 1) 263 1614.
Petőfi Csarnok
Venue for many famous concerts.
Zichy Mihály utca 14.
Tel: (06 1) 251 7266.

Floor Shows
Caligula
The name's promise of decadent entertainment draws the cognoscenti.
Szilágyi Erzsébet fasor 37–39.
Tel: (06 1) 212 3177.
Open: 10pm–5am.
Moulin Rouge
Nagymező utca 10.
Tel: (06 1) 269 0991.

Jazz

Attempts are being made to stimulate the jazz scene which languished under Communism. An excellent initiative by the municipality was the founding of the Merlin Theatre and Jazz Café in 1990. The most enduringly popular local ensemble is the Benkó Dixieland Band.

Hades Jazz Club
Equipped with a fine bar, this place also calls itself a 'jazztaurant'.
Vörüsmarty utca 31.
Tel: (06 1) 352 1503.
Open: Mon–Fri
noon–2am, Sat–Sun
5pm–2am.

Jazz Garden
Authentic modern and swing.
Veres Pálné utca 44/A.
Tel: (06 1) 266 7364.
Open: Mon–Thu
10pm–1am, Fri till 2am,
Sat 6pm–2am, Sun
1pm–1am.

Merlin Jazz Club
Restaurant in Merlin Theatre. Local and foreign stars appear.
Gerlóczy utca 4.
Tel: (01) 317 9338.
Performances at 10pm and
midnight, Fri–Sun.

Rock

Old Man's Pub
Akácfa utca 13.
Tel: (06 1) 322 7645.

Open: daily 3pm–4am.
Rolling Rock Café
Live music until the early hours.
Bécsi út 53–55.
Tel: (01) 368 2298.
Open: until 5am.

Rocktogon
Full of youthful trendies.
Mozsár utca 9.
Tel: (01) 353 0443.
Open: Tue–Sat 7pm–4am.

For nightlife happenings, see the listings in the style section of the *Budapest Sun*, and the local weekly programme of events, *Pesti Műsor* (in Hungarian, published Thursdays). The Tourist Board issues a monthly *Programme* in English.

A typical floor show, Pest-style

Children

The suggestions below are for activities largely unaffected by the language barrier. Parents could also consider a visit to a stalactite cave or the Buda Hills (*see p135*) or, in summer, a boat trip on the Danube.

The Big Wheel, Luna Park

Bábszinház (Puppet Show)
Shows are based mainly on international and Hungarian fairy tales.
Andrássy út 69. Tel: (06 1) 321 5200.
Ticket office open: daily 9am–6pm.
Metro: toVörösmarty utca.

Csodák Palotája (Palace of Miracles)
Central Europe's first interactive scientific playhouse has over 100 games, experiments, and many visual effects.
Váci út 19. Tel: (06 1) 6131;
www.csodapalota.hu Open: Mon–Fri
9am–5pm, Sat & Sun 10am–6pm.
Metro: to Lehel tér.

Gellért Gyógyfürdő (Gellért Baths)
There are many baths (*see pp36–7*) but Gellért offers the bubble bath inside and the wave bath outside.

Gyermekvasút (Children's Railway)
Formerly the 'Pioneer Railway' of the Communist youth movement, running 12km between Széchenyi-hegy and Hűvösvölgy in the Buda Hills, it has been temporarily saved but its future is uncertain. The driver is adult but the staff are children (compulsory retirement age, 14).
See also p135.
Széchenyi-hegy is reached by the Fogaskerekű Vasút (cogwheel railway), whose terminus is opposite Hotel Budapest, Szilágyi Erzsébet fasor 47.

Kölyökpark (Kidpark)
Five hundred square metres of indoor play facilities for children under 12.
Fóti út 81/B. Tel: (06 1) 399 2059.
Open: daily 10am–8pm. Bus: red No. 20 from Keleti pályaudvar, black No. 20 from Újpest-Központ metro station.

Margit Sziget (Margaret Island)
The various sights are described on pages 44–5. For children, bicycles, and tricycles can be hired at the southern end, next to the Centennial Monument. At the northern end is the Japanese Garden

Luna Park in Városliget has plenty to occupy children

with its waterfall and a 'singing well' that plays a tune each hour.

Museums

Bélyegmúzeum (Stamp Museum)
Eleven million stamps!
Hársfa utca 47. Tel: (06 1) 341 5526.
Open: Tue–Sun 10am–6pm (until 4pm
Nov–Mar). Admission charge.
Trolley bus: 74.

Füsti Magyar Vasúttörténti Park
(Hungarian Railway History Park)
Over a hundred railway vehicles on view.
Tatai út 95. Tel: (06 1)428 0180;
www.lokopark.hu Open: Apr–Oct,
Tue–Sun 10am–6pm; Nov, Dec, & Mar,
Tue–Sun 10am–3pm. Closed: Jan & Feb.
Bus: 30 from Keleti pályaudvar, special
trains from the Nyugati Railway Station
in the summer.

Postsai és Távközlési Múzeum
(Postal Museum)
Models, coaches, and a message despatch tube to play with.
Andrássy út 3. Tel: (06 1) 269 6838.
Open: Tue–Sun 10am–6pm (until 4pm
Nov–Mar) Admission charge. Metro: to
Bajcsy-Zsilinszky út.

Telefónia Múzeum
(Telephone Museum)
Children can play with the exhibits.
Úri utca 49. Tel: (06 1) 201 8188.
Open: Tue–Sun 10am–5.30pm (until 4pm
Nov–Mar). Admission charge. Várbusz to
Szentháromság tér.
See also Museums pp72–9.

Planetárium

Laser and special shows for children.
Népliget. Tel: (06 1) 265 0725.
Times of shows vary. Admission charge.
Metro: to Népliget.

Play Areas

Play areas are scarce on the Buda side, but one worth considering is Nagy Imre tér off Fö utca and the one in the new Millenáris Park behind the Mamut shopping centre. On the Pest side is the secluded Károlyi kert behind the Károlyi Palace. Erzsébet tér is well equipped with climbing bars, sand-pits, etc and other lots of other fun activities.

Tropicarium

This has the distinction of being the largest aquarium in central Europe.
Nagytétényi út 37–45. Tel: (06 1) 424
3053; www.tropicarium.hu Open: daily
10am–8pm. Tétény-busz fast bus line
from Szent Gellért tér, or black No. 3 from
Móricz Zsigmond körtér.

Városliget (City Woodland Park)
Állatkert (Zoo)
Three thousand animals and a special children's corner.
Állatkerti körút 6–12. Tel: (06 1) 363
3710. Open: 9am–6pm (4pm in winter).

Fövárosi Nagycirkusz (Circus)
Állatkerti körút 7. Tel: (06 1) 343 8300.
Shows: Wed–Fri 3pm & 7pm, Sat–Sun
10am & 3pm. Closed: Mon, Tue & 1
Sep–mid-Oct.

Vidám Park (Amusement Park)
Állatkerti körút 14-16. Tel: (06 1) 363
8310; www.vidampark.hu Open: Apr–Sep
10am–8pm, Oct–Mar 10am–7pm.
Closed: Nov–Feb. Separate section for
small children.

Trolley bus 72 from the metro stop at
Arany János utca or metro to Széchenyi
fürdő brings you close to all three of the
above locations.

Sport and Leisure

Magyars are great football fans and Hungary has produced some charismatic players like Puskás. Otherwise they excel in sports such as swimming and water polo, no doubt helped by the top-class training facilities available.

This way to the swimming baths

SPECTATOR SPORTS
Cycle Racing
There is a championship track with a capacity of 14,000 for cycle-racing enthusiasts.
Millenáris Cycle Track, Stefánia út 2. Tel: (06 1) 251 1222. Bus 7.

Football
International matches are held in the Népstadion (Istvánmezei út 3–7, *tel: (06 1) 251 1222*), which holds 76,000 spectators. The two leading Budapest teams are Ferencvárosi Torna Club (FTC), whose ground is at Üllői út 129 (*tel: (06 1) 215 6025*; metro to Népliget), and Kispest-Honvéd (Új temető út 1–3; *tel: (06 1) 282 9789*; tram 42 from the metro stop at Határ út). Matches are played at weekends and on Wednesday evenings. Information from the monthly *Programme* obtainable at Tourinform, Sütő utca 2, or Vöröomarly tér (Vigadió utca).

Horse Racing
Flat racing (*galopp*) takes place at Kincsem Park, Albertirsai út 2 (*tel: (06 1) 263 7818*; metro to Pillangó utca) on Sundays between March and November. Trotting races (*ügető*) take place at Ügetőpalya, Kerepesi út 9 (*tel: (06 1) 313 9915*; bus 95; trolley bus 80 from Keleti pályaudvar) at 2pm on Saturdays, 4pm on Wednesdays. Details in *Programme*. Punters may place bets at the tote.

Hungarian Grand Prix
The Grand Prix is held annually in early August at the Mogyoród circuit, 24km northeast of Budapest (reached by car on the M3 motorway; bus terminus varies yearly, make sure you check). Tourinform and English language newspapers carry details.

SPORTS FACILITIES
Aerobics
Andi Studio
Hold utca 29. Tel: (06 1) 311 0740.
Astoria Fitness Centre
Károly körút 4. Tel: (06 1) 317 0452.

Bowling
Strike Bowling Club
Budafoki út 111–13.
Tel: (06 1) 206 2754.
Vilati Bowling Club
in the Duna Plaza, Váci út 178.
Tel: (061) 239 3829.

Cycling
Hungarian roads are dangerous for cyclists, but efforts are being made to create cycle paths. Tourinform should have a map of routes (*Budapest Kerék-*

párútjai). Bicycle shops include Bike Cserny Shop and Service (Zuhatag sor 12, *tel: (061) 200 6837*) and Rokon Bicycle (Mátyás Kitály út 6, *tel: (06 1) 250 3038*).

Fishing

Not allowed between 20 April and 20 May. The Danube and Tisza hold carp, pike, and many other species. Contact MOHOSZ (Hungarian Fishing Association, Korompai utca 17; *tel: (06 1) 319 9790*) for information and permits. Daily tickets are available.

Golf

Budapest Golfpark és Country Club Bt
On Szentendre Island. For details, contact the city office.
Bécsi utca 5. Tel: (06 1) 317 2749.
The 19th Hole Centrum
Nádor utca 32. Tel: (06 1) 265 1247.

Horse Racing

Budapesti Lovas Klub
In the city; has a huge hall for winter exercise.
Kerepesi út 7. Tel: (06 1) 313 5210.
Petneházy Country Club
Riding in the hills. Lessons available for all levels.
Feketefej utca 2–4. Tel: (06 1) 275 7276.

Running

The Budapest Marathon is usually held in the spring over a route between Népstadion and Római fürdő Registration at IBUSZ on Ferenciek tere.

Swimming

The choice is enormous (*see pp36–7*). Sports pools include:

Hajós Alfréd Nemzeti Sportuszoda (Alfréd Hajós Sport Pool)
Margit Sziget. Tel: (06 1) 340 4946.
Open: Mon–Fri 6am–6pm, weekends 6am–2pm. (Competitions may restrict public use.)
Nyéki Imre Uszoda (Imre Nyéki Swimming Pool)
Large 33m, 8-lane pool; 27°C.
Kondorosi út 14. Tel: (06 1) 208 4025.
Open: Mon–Fri 6am–8pm, weekends 6am–5pm.

Squash

Top Squash Club
In the Mammut shopping mall; also has a sauna and bowling.
Széna tér. Tel: (06 1) 345 8193.

Tennis

There are over 30 tennis clubs, but many are a long way out. It may be easier to opt for a hotel court. Try:
Flamenco Hotel – *Tas vezér utca 7.*
Tel: (06 1) 372 2000.
Grand Hotel Hungaria – *Rákóczi út 90.*
Tel: (06 1) 478 1100.
Tusculanum Hotel – *Záhony utca 10.*
Tel: (06 1) 388 7673.

Enthusiastic future stars

Dog Days in Budapest

Non-experts could be forgiven for looking blank at the mention of an *agár*, a *puli*, a *pumi*, or a *mudi*. All of them are high-performance canines bred by a people with a passion for working dogs.

The classic Hungarian breeds are believed to have accompanied the seven Magyar tribes across the Carpathians 1,100 years ago. Of these, the shaggy black *puli*, which looks like an animated hearthrug, is something of a national symbol. It is still unrivalled for rounding up sheep at pasture. Something bigger was needed to keep predators at bay, and this task was performed by the bulky *komondors* and *kuvasz* (easily distinguishable from wolves and other marauders by their white colour).

The beautiful *vizsla*, a ginger-coloured retriever, was kept by the Árpád kings as early as the 11th century, and the greyhound-like *agár* (also of Asian origin) was used for deer-hunting by the nobility.

Dog-fanciers can now spot (or buy) Hungarian and other breeds at the twice-yearly dog sale on Marczibányi tér. In the early days of Communism luxury breeds were virtually banned, and vets would only attend working animals. Now, dogs are once again a status symbol – and often a protection against burglars.

The European Dog Show was held in May 1993 in the Sportcsarnok of the Népstadion, proving that Budapest is back on the international canine map. Exhibitors came from 14 countries, including the USA and Russia, to this annual event where the fate of 6,000 glamorous dogs was decided by a

panel of international judges. In a world of economic gloom and general disillusionment the dog-show arouses enormous enthusiasm; Hungarians, it seems, are happy to share the view of the Marquise de Sévigné, who once observed: 'The more I see of men, the more I admire dogs'.

Hungary is truly a nation of dog lovers; most people own dogs as pets and there are also many breeds of working dogs, such as the *puli* on the right

Food and Drink

As in other cities of the former Eastern Bloc, the catering business enjoyed a boom following the collapse of Communism. New restaurants have mushroomed, old-established ones have been given a face-lift. Foreign investment has affected every area, but fast-food, beer cellars, and the luxury end of the market have benefited especially from new capital.

Fresh or conserved, Hungarian produce is of excellent quality

The better class restaurants should be booked in advance, at least for an evening. Bear in mind that you will need a taxi for reaching some of the attractive restaurants in outlying areas like the Buda Hills – it is forbidden to drive in Hungary with any alcohol in the blood.

Types of Eating House

There are three main categories of eating house: an *étterem* offers a large selection of dishes and can be any price category; a *vendéglő* should offer something more like home cooking with fewer dishes to choose from, and also tends to have more ambience. *Vendéglő* prices used to be more moderate, but

Hungarian wines are made from some of the world's most succulent grapes

many have been subjected to the same sort of gentrification as similar establishments in other countries, which invariably means higher prices. A *csárda* is a country-style inn with a relatively restricted menu and simple fare. Smaller establishments with cheaper prices are called *bisztró* or, if self-service, *önkiszolgáló* or *ételbár*. A *söröző* is a beer cellar, which usually serves (fairly basic) food; a few are like ordinary restaurants.

HUNGARIAN CUISINE

Most people's idea of Hungarian cooking begins and ends with 'goulash', a dish that in Hungary itself bears little resemblance to the anaemic version served elsewhere. We think of it as a stew, but it is just as likely to be encountered as a rich meaty soup (*gulyásleves*). The origins of *gulyáshús* lie in the nomadic period of the Magyars; their horsemen would often travel for days in hostile terrain carrying iron rations of stewed mutton or beef, dried and preserved in a bag made from a sheep's stomach. To prepare a meal they would simply soften the meat in boiling water, creating a sort of instant stew. It is believed that this contributed to the success of their campaigns – the enemy had to waste time killing and cooking their food.

There is a great deal more to Hungarian cuisine than 'goulash', however. Hungary's geographical position ensured that surrounding cultures had an impact on its cooking: Balkan influence is seen in the stuffed vegetables; the sausage culture (although very ancient) has been modified by German and Italian practices; and dumplings were borrowed from the Slavs. The lands of historic Hungary had their own regional dishes, such as tarragon lamb stew from Transylvania and *lecsó* (peppers and tomatoes stewed in lard) from southern Hungary.

The basis of most Hungarian food preparation is a heavy roux of pork lard and flour, known as *rántás*, liberally spiced, usually with paprika. Many dishes include sour cream or slices of smoked sausage, thus creating the characteristic combination of astringent and smoky tastes.

Pork (*sertés*) is the most frequent meat on the menu, usually in some kind of *pörkölt* (stew). Beef (*marha*) is not common and is seldom good quality, with one striking exception: Budapestians are fanatic consumers of Steak Tartar, and many restaurants serve it with all the trappings. Lamb (*bárány*, *birka*) is hard to come by – you are more likely to encounter it in country inns.

Soups (*leves*) play a major role in Hungarian cooking. In summer an excellent cold sour cherry soup (*meggyleves*) is often on offer, while fish restaurants serve a fish soup (*halászlé*), the speciality of Szeged in southern Hungary. Freshwater fish (carp, pike, perch) from the Danube, the Tisza, and Lake Balaton can be good, although it is best to order a fillet if you dislike coping with bones. The best fish is undoubtedly *fogas* (pike-perch): the Gundel chef serves it with cream-cheese sauce on a bed of spinach, when it is well-nigh irresistible. More mundane are the meat and poultry dishes fried in breadcrumbs (*rántott hús, rántott csirke*), like a Wiener Schnitzel. Chicken paprika (*paprikás csirke*), prepared with paprika spice and sour cream, provides the tongue-tingling flavours the Magyars love. Vegetables come either stuffed (*töltött*), like cabbage or peppers, or in a *fözelék*, a delicious semi-purée (the one made with marrow – *tökfőelék* – is especially good).

The choice of puddings tends to be rather limited, perhaps because Hungarians with a sweet tooth are well catered for by pastry shops and cafés; however, pancakes (especially the version stuffed with curds – *túró*) are a nice way to round off a meal. A sponge confection with chocolate sauce and whipped cream (*somlói galuska*) is held in affection by the locals.

Baroness Orczy

Baroness Orczy, famed authoress of *The Scarlet Pimpernel* (1905), lived much of her life in England, although she was of Hungarian origin. Asked to compare the lifestyle of the two countries, she replied: 'I would say the Englishman lives like a king and eats like a pig; and the Hungarian lives like a pig, but God knows he eats like a king!'

MENU READER

ELŐETELEK	**(HORS D'OEUVRES)**	**KÉSZÉTELEK**	**(READY DISHES)**
gombafejek		**borjú pörkölt**	veal stew
rántva	fried mushrooms	**sertés pörkölt**	pork stew
hortobágyi	meat pancake with	**töltött káposzta**	stuffed cabbage
palacsinta	sour cream	**töltött paprika**	stuffed pepper
libamáj	goose liver		

		FRISSENSÜLTEK	**(DISHES PREPARE**
LEVESEK	**(SOUPS)**		**TO ORDER)**
bableves	bean soup	**Halételek**	(fish)
gulyásleves	goulash soup	**Balatoni fogas**	Balaton pike-
halászlé	fishermen's broth		perch
meggyleves	sour cherry soup	**csuka**	pike
		ponty rántva	fried carp
		süllő	young pike-perch

HÚSÉTELEK	**(MEAT)**
fatányéros	mixed grill
magyaros tál	fried meat and
	vegetables
sertésmáj	pig's liver

SZÁRNYASOK	**(POULTRY)**
kacsa	duck
liba	goose
paprikás csirke	paprika chicken

VADAK/	
VADMADARAK	**(GAME)**
fácán	pheasant
fogoly	partridge
nyúl	hare
őzhús/szarvashús	venison
vaddisznó	wild boar
vadkacsa	wild duck
vadliba	wild goose

Dried paprika, chillies, and garlic

TÉSZTÁK	(PASTA/RICE)
galuska	small dumplings
káposztás kocka	pasta with cabbage
rizs	rice
tarhonya	pasta grains
túrós csusza	pasta layers with
	cottage cheese

GOMBÓCOK	(DUMPLINGS)
barackos gombóc	apricot dumpling
szilvás gombóc	plum dumpling

FŐZELÉK	(VEGETABLES)
burgonya	potato
hasábburgonya	French fries
főtt krumpli	boiled potatoes
sült krumpli	roast potatoes
fokhagyma	garlic
hagyma	onion
káposzta	cabbage
zöldbabfőzelék	French beans
zöldpaprika	green pepper

SALÁTÁK	(SALADS)
fejes saláta	lettuce
káposztasaláta	cabbage salad
paradicsom	tomato
savanyúság	pickles
uborkasaláta	cucumber salad
(vizes) uborka	gherkin

ÉDESSÉGEK	(DESSERTS)
fagylalt	ice-cream
gesztenye püré	chestnut purée
Gundel' palacsinta	pancake with
	chocolate sauce and
	ground walnuts

GYÜMÖLCSÖK	(FRUIT)
alma	apple
banán	banana
citrom	lemon
cseresznye	cherry
meggy	Morello cherry
eper	strawberry
körte	pear
málna	raspberry
narancs	orange
őszibarack	peach
(sárga) barack	apricot
szilva	plum

ITALOK	(DRINKS)
fehér bor	white wine
vörös bor	red wine
édes	sweet
száraz	dry
pezsgő	'champagne'
	(usually Sekt)
likör	liqueur
pálinka	
schnapps	(fruit-based)
csapolt sör	draught beer
dobozos sör	canned beer
üveges sör	bottled beer
üditők	soft drinks
szénsavmentes	still mineral
dsvanyvíz	water
szénsavas	sparkling mineral
dsvanyvíz	water
szódavíz	soda water
jég	ice
gyümölcslé	fruit juice
kávé	coffee
tea citrommal	tea with lemon
tejes tea	tea with milk

Where to Eat

Prices for all restaurants are quoted in four categories which should be taken as guidelines rather than exact figures. Average meal prices per head are given, excluding drinks and service (customarily 10 per cent). Service is not included unless stated on the menu-card. Inflation in Hungary is around 7–8 per cent, so expect price rises.

★	up to 1000 Ft (fast-food, snack bars, etc)
★★	up to 2,000 Ft
★★★	up to 3,000 Ft
★★★★	over 3,000 Ft

Hungarian

Apostolok ★★★
Marvellous 1920s' interior invoking the shades of historic Hungary. Excellent service and traditional Hungarian dishes.
Kigyó utca 4–6.
Tel: (06 1) 267 0290.
Open: daily 10am–midnight. Metro: to Ferenciek tere.

Aranyszarvas ★★★★
A famous game restaurant in a Neo-Classical house in the Tabán. Mouth-watering wild boar stew and pheasant. Reasonably

restrained gypsy band.
Szarvas tér 1. Tel: (06 1) 375 6451. Open: daily 6pm–midnight. Buses: 5 & 85 to Szarvas tér.

Bagolyvár ★★★
Part of the Gundel empire, but cheaper. It concentrates on a few traditional dishes changed on a daily basis.
Állatkerti út 2.
Tel: (06 1) 468 3110.
Open: daily noon–11pm.
Metro: to Hősök tere.

Camelot ★★★
Medieval dining and ambience.
Benczúr uta 15.
Tel: (06 1) 351 9472.
Open: noon –midnight.
Closed: Sun.

Csarnok É Herem ★★
A very popular, typical Hungarian eating place with outside seating in summer.
Hold utca 11. Tel: (06 1) 269 4906. Trolley bus: 70 & 78 to Honvéd utca.

Csendes ★★
Friendly service, good value. Transylvanian specialities. Ideal for lunch.
Múzeum körút 13.
Tel: (06 1) 267 0218.
Open: Mon–Sat noon–midnight.
Metro: to Astoria.

Gundel ★★★★
Hungarian *haute cuisine*

Inside a cellar restaurant

in elegant surroundings. The most famous restaurant in Hungary. Refurbished by New York restaurateur of Hungarian origin, George Lang, it has regained its former *belle époque* glory. Reservations essential.
Állatkerti út 2. Tel: (06 1) 468 4040. Open: daily noon–3pm, 7pm–midnight. Metro: to Hősök tere

Kéhli Vendéglő ★★★
Really excellent Hungarian cooking; aficionados rave about the bone marrow served in a red pot.
Mókus utca 22 (Óbuda).
Tel: (06 1) 250 4241 Open weekdays 5pm–midnight, weekends from noon. Near the Aquincum Hotel.

Kispipa Vendéglő ★★★
Famous for its incredibly long and illegible menu. Inter-war ambience, old-

fashioned service. Reserve ahead.
Akácfa utca 38. Tel: (06 1) 342 2587. Open: Mon–Sat noon–1am. Trams: 4 & 6 to Wesselényi utca.

Mátyás Pince ★★★★
Excellent fish and poultry; very popular with tourists. The best-known gypsy band plays here. Reserve ahead.
Március 15 tér 7.
Tel: (06 1) 318 1693.
Open: daily 11am–1am.
Metro: to Ferenciek tere.

Náncsi Néni Vendéglője ★★★
Attractive outdoor location. Rather heavy

food but some unusual specialities, eg cottage cheese dumplings.
Ördögárok utca 80.
Tel: (06 1) 397 2742.
Open: daily noon–11pm.
Far out in Hűvösvölgy – take a taxi.

Sipos Halászkert ★★★
If you want to try fishermen's broth (*halászlé*), pike-perch (*fogas*) or carp (*ponty*), this could be the place for you. Balaton white wines to wash it down.
Fő tér 6 (Óbuda).
Tel: (01) 388 8745.
Open: daily noon–11pm.
HÉV to Árpád híd.

Tabáni Kakas Vendéglő ★★★
The chef stresses that almost all dishes are cooked with goose fat, not lard. The chicken casserole is much praised.
Attila út 27. Tel: (01) 375 7165. Open: daily noon–midnight. Buses: 5 & 85 to Szarvas tér.

Tüköry Söröző ★★
A place for steak Tartar buffs. Home cooking, engagingly shabby decor.
Hold utca 15.
Tel: (01) 269 5027.
Open: Mon–Fri 10am–midnight. Metro: to Arany János utca.

In summer Budapestians prefer to eat al fresco

Paprika and Pálinka

The Hungarian temperament is often said to be ardent and volatile, qualities that are mirrored in the national taste for hot spice (*paprika*) and fiery spirits (*pálinka*). The most famous of the firewaters is apricot schnapps (*Barack-pálinka*), the best of which is distilled on the Alföld (Great Hungarian Plain) at Kecskemét. It is made from two varieties of apricot, the *kajszi* and the more juicy *rakovsky*, which has a strong aroma. The crushed stones of the apricots are added to the juice, and the liquid is fermented in oak barrels for at least a year. The best barack is sold in bottles with a white label featuring a picture of the Kecskemét town hall. Some *barack* comes in traditional long-necked flasks known as 'whistlers' (*fütyülő*) or in a *kulacs* made of Herend porcelain. The Hungarian custom is to down your *pálinka* in one gulp, which can be disconcerting, especially as it is usually drunk on an empty stomach as an aperitif.

Paprika, or capsicum, was probably introduced into Hungary in the 16th century by the Bulgarian retainers of the Turks (Bulgarians were traditionally great horticulturists). The poorer classes began using it as a condiment, a habit that spread to the nobility in the 19th century. The great Hungarian biochemist, Albert Szent-Györgyi, stumbled on capsicum's curative properties by accident, when working at Szeged University. He hated paprika, but his wife was convinced it was good for him and packed some in his luncheon box every day. Unable to eat it, he decided instead to see what it contained; his analysis led him to the discovery of Vitamin C – and a Nobel Prize.

Paprika is grown all over Hungary, but the best is said to come from Szeged and Kalocsa in the south. In this region you can see the decorative strings of paprika pods hung out to dry on the verandas of peasant houses. There are several different types: a small and hot

DISHES WITH PAPRIKA

All kinds of pörkölt (stew) (see p161)
Halászlé (fish soup)
paprikás csirke (paprika chicken)
hortobágyi husos palacsinta
(meat pancake filled with stew)
gulyásleves (goulash soup)
paprikás krumpli (paprika potatoes).

red one, a large sweeter red version, a green one and the succulent yellow, ideal for eating raw with salami. Almost all typically Hungarian soups and main dishes are spiced with paprika.

. . . without which no Hungarian meal is complete

Chinese restaurant

International/ Continental Cuisine

Légrádi Tsetvérek ★★★★
International cuisine with a French flavour and some Hungarian dishes. Reservation essential.
Magyar utca 23.
Tel: (06 1) 318 6804.
Open: Mon–Sat
6pm–midnight.
Metro: to Astoria.
The above is the Légrádi Brothers' restaurant. Irén Légrádi has opened an equally stylish establishment at nearby Bárczy István utca 3–5.
Tel: (06 1) 266 4993.

Robinson ★★★★
Attractively located on a raft on the lake of Városliget (City Woodland Park). Carefully chosen menu of international and Hungarian dishes. Guitar music.
Városligeti tó, Állatkerti körút 1. Tel: (06 1) 422 1224. Open: daily noon–4pm, 6pm–midnight (weekends dinner only).
Metro: to Hősök tere.

Vadrózsa ★★★★
The most fashionable restaurant in town, situated in a Baroque villa on the Rózsadomb. Extremely expensive set price meal, no menu, and no wine list (the waiter advises). Terrace in summer.
Pentelei Molnár utca 15.
Tel: (06 1) 326 5817.
Open: Tue–Sun
6pm–midnight.
Bus: 91 to Vérhalom tér, or take a taxi.

American

Chicago Rib Shack Restaurant ★★★
Ribs, burgers, and drinkable draught beer. Very friendly service.
Szent István körút 2.
Tel: (06 1) 302 3112.
Open: daily noon–1am.
Metro: to Nyugati

pálavaudvar; Trams: 2, 2A, 4 & 6; buses: 6, 15, 26, 91, & 191.

Iguana Restaurant
Mexican food.
Zoltán utca. Tel: 331 4352.
Open: daily 11.30am–midnight. Trams: 2 & 2A; trolley bus: 70 & 78 to Kossuth Ljos tér.

Rolling Rock Café ★★
American-style eatery with American and Mexican fare.
Bécsi út 53–55.
Tel: (01) 368 2298.
Tram: 17 to Kolosy tér.

Chinese

Nefrit ★★★
Excellent cuisine, great ambience.
Apor Vilmos tér.
Tel: (06 1) 213 9039.
Open: noon–midnight.
Bus: 105; tram: 59.

Xi-Hu ★★★
Authentic flavours from different parts of China.
Nádor utca 5.
Tel (06 1) 337 5697.
Open: noon–midnight.
Bus: 15, or citybusz.

Czech

Svejk ★★★
Cheerful atmosphere; big portions of Czech and Slovak specialities. Handy for the Music Academy.
Király utca 59b.
Tel: (06 1) 322 3278.

*Open: daily noon–11pm.
Trams: 4, 6 to Király utca.*

French
Le Jardin de Paris ★★★★
Bistro-style atmospheric
restaurant with French
wines on offer – at a
price. Late-night opening
with live jazz in the
evenings.
*Fő utca 20. Tel: (06 1) 201
0047. Open: daily
noon–midnight.
Metro: to Batthyány tér.*

German
**Kaltenberg Royal
Bavarian Brasserie ★★**
Bavarian food in portions
that leave you over full.
*Kinizsi utca 30–36.
Tel: (06 1) 215 9792.
Open: noon–midnight.
Metro: to Ferenc körút;
trams: 4 & 6 to Üllői út.*

Greek
**Jorgosz Greek
Taverna ★★★**
Authentic decor, music,
and food in a Pest cellar.
*Csengery utca 24.
Tel: (06 1) 341 0772.
Open: daily 11am–11pm.
Metro: to Vörösmarty
utca.*

Italian
Kis Itália ★★
Excellent pizzas and
pasta; good service.

*Szemere utca 22.
Tel: (06 1) 269 3145.
Open: Mon–Sat
11am–9pm. Metro: to
Kossuth Lajos tér.*

Marco Polo ★★★★
Claimed by some to offer
the best food (of any
kind) in the city. Prices
match the claim.
*Vigadó tér 3.
Tel: (06 1) 338 3925.
Open: daily noon–3pm,
7.30pm–midnight.
Tram 2 to Vigadó tér.*

Japanese
**Fuji Japan
Restaurant ★★★★**
In a pagoda-like interior
where enthusiasts can
watch the chef at work.
*Csatárka utca 54/B. Tel:
(06 1) 325 7111. Open:
noon–11pm. Bus: 11 from
Batthyány tér metro.*

Jewish
Carmel Pince ★★★
Kosher specialities in
pleasant surroundings.
Very popular, so reserve.
*Kazinczy utca 31.
Tel: (06 1) 342 4585.
Open: daily noon–11pm.
Metro: to Astoria.*

Korean
**Senara Korean
Restaurant ★★★**
The cheaper of

Budapest's two Korean
restaurants, but just as
authentic.
*Dohány utca 5.
Tel: (06 1) 269 6549.
Open: daily 11.30am–
2.30pm, 6–11pm.
Metro: to Astoria.*

Vegetarian
Vegetárium ★★★
All there is for vegetarians
in the city, apart from
salad bars. Has a good
reputation among the
*cognoscenti.
Cukor utca 3.
Tel: (06 1) 484 0848.
Open: daily noon–11pm.
Metro: to Ferenciek tere.*

Pizzas have arrived in a big way

Beer halls are good value and the choice of foreign beer is increasing all the time

Sörözok (Beer Halls)

Budapest beer cannot compare with Czech or German brews, which are luckily increasingly available in the capital. Austrian beer (particularly the ubiquitous Gösser) is also common, due to heavy Austrian investment in Hungarian breweries.

Becketts Irish Bar ★★
Authentic Irish pub with live entertainment. Voted the best in 1995–6.
Bajcsy–Zsilinszky út 72.
Tel: (01) 311 1003.
Open: noon–1am.
Metro: to Nyugati páyaudvar.

John Bull Pub ★★★
English beer and food, but expensive and for those who cannot survive without their pint.
Apáczai Csere János utca 17. Tel: (06 1) 318 6847. Open: daily noon–midnight.
Tram: 2 to Eötrös tér.

Pilsner Urquell ★★★
Prices reflect Váci utca location, but it is handy for a shopper's lunch.
Váci utca 15.
Tel: (06 1) 318 3814.
Open: daily 10am–11pm.
Metro: to Ferenciek tere.

Söröző a Szent Jupáthoz ★★
Beer cellar offering figure-destroying fare round the clock.
Retek utca 16.
Tel: (06 1) 212 2923.
Open: 24 hours.
Metro: to Moszkva tér.

Kavezok, Cukraszdak (Cafés, Cake Shops)

Some coffee houses miraculously survived the kill-joy ethos of Communism and are now enthusiastically recapturing the spirit of a more leisured age.

Angelika ★
A favourite meeting place on the Buda side, cosy in winter, cool in summer on the terrace.
Batthyány tér 7.
Tel: (06 1) 212 3784.
Open: daily 10am–10pm.
Metro: to Batthyány tér.

Central Kavehaz ★★
Recently renovated to recall its late-19th century days of glory. This popular café also serves lunch and dinner.
Károlyi Mihály utca 9.
Tel: (06 1) 266 4572.
Open: 8am–midnight.
Bus: 7, 15, 78, 173; citybusz to Ferenciek tere; trams: 2 & 2A.

Gerbeaud ★★
The most famous of Pest's cafés since Swiss patissier, Emil Gerbeaud, took it over in 1883. Period interior, excellent pastries (which you can also take away).
Vörösmarty tér 7.
Tel: (06 1) 429 9000.
Open: daily 9am–9pm.
Metro: to Vörösmarty tér.

Lukács ★
Said to have the best
pastries in town. Nostalgic
atmosphere and decor.
Andrássy út 79.
Tel: (06 1) 302 8747.
Open: daily 9am–8pm.
Metro: to Oktogon.

Művész ★
Delightful early-20th
century interior. Usually
full of musicians and
artistes.
Andrássy út 29.
Tel: (06 1) 352 1337.
*Open: daily 9am–mid-
night. Metro: to Opera.*

Ruszwurm ★
A famous and charming
café with original
Biedermeier cherrywood
furnishings. The cream
slice (*krémes*) is the best
in town.
Szentháromság utca 7.
Tel: (06 1) 375 5284.
Open: daily 10am–7pm.
*Várbusz: to
Szentháromság tér.*

Fast-Food
The range has expanded
enormously in recent
years. Try the following:

Jégbüfé Cukrászda ★
Very convenient for that
fresh pastry and quick
coffee.
Ferenciek tere 10.
Tel: (061) 318 3271.

Open: 8am–6pm.
Metro: to Ferenciek tere.

McDonald's ★
The one at the Western
Railway Station (Nyugati
pályaudvar) has a
classic interior; it is
more convenient to go
those Régiposta utca (just
off Váci utca) and Süto
utca (next to
Tourinform).
Open: 9am–10pm.

Szeráj ★
Self-service Turkish
canteen.
Szent István körút 13.
Open: 9am–4am.
*Metro: to Nyugati
pályaudvar.*

The most famous cake shop in Hungary, Gerbeaud, is in this huge building

Wines of Hungary

To wine buffs familiar only with the much-promoted *Egri Bikaver* (Bulls' Blood from Eger), Hungarian viticulture offers the prospect of interesting discoveries. The country has 16 wine-growing regions producing many refreshing and somewhat acidic white wines, together with a number of full-bodied reds. Most Hungarian wine is drunk young, and over-production of poor quality plonk is endemic, made worse by the collapse of the huge Russian market. (Asked why he did not export the resultant surplus elsewhere, one producer gravely replied:

'Because it is unfit for human consumption.')

To learn about the better quality wines one could do worse than visit the Magyar Borok Háza (House of Hungarian wines) where there is a choice of 1,000 wines from all regions and tasting is possible (Szentháromság tér 6, Castle Hill, *tel: (06 1) 212 1030; www.kertnet.hu/mbh* Open: daily noon–8pm).

The best white wines come from the volcanic Badacsony plateau on the northern shore of Lake Balaton, from Gyöngyös in northern Hungary, and from the Tokaji Hills, although there is also extensive production on the Great Plain. Native grapes like Hárslevelű (Lime Leaf) or Furmint from Tokaj produce pleasantly drinkable wines, while Szürkebarát (Pinot Gris) and Olaszrizling (Italian Riesling) are good Balaton products. The best reds come from the Villány region of southern Hungary, whose Cabernet Sauvignons and Merlots are occasionally outstanding.

Uniquely Hungarian is the famous golden dessert wine, Tokaji Aszú – 'the wine of kings and king of wines'. The region in northeastern Hungary where it is produced has undergone upheaval because of privatisation and ownership disputes, but the honeyed nectar is still available. Once you have tried it you will understand the enthusiasm of Pope Benedict who wrote to thank Maria Theresa for a consignment in

the 18th century and delivered a graceful eulogy of Tokaji: 'Blessed is the land that produced you, blessed the lady who sent you; and blessed am I who drink you.'

After years of concentrating on quantity, some Hungarian suppliers are now focusing on producing top quality wines

Hotels and Accommodation

Budapest is exceptional in having tackled the shortage of hotel accommodation much sooner than other former Eastern Bloc capitals. The 55,000 beds of 1989 have been considerably added to and new hotels are still opening, albeit at a slower rate. These must cater for around five million visitors annually. Availability can be strained at peak times (mid-summer, when the Grand Prix is held, Christmas, and New Year).

The luxurious Grand Hotel Corvinus Kempinski

Those who can be more flexible than businessmen in a hurry should have little problem finding accommodation, providing they are happy to consider staying in the private rooms that double the bed supply at peak periods. For hotels it is vital to book in advance from abroad if you want a specific location or facility (for example, a Danube view or a quiet room not overlooking a main thoroughfare).

You should bear in mind that mid-price hotels may have taken block bookings from tour operators up to a year in advance; there remains a shortage of this sort of accommodation because of the obsession of developers with profitable luxury hotels.

Prices

As elsewhere in Eastern Europe the standards prevailing in any given star category may not always match up to the expectations of Western visitors, though this mostly applies to older establishments in the upper mid-price bracket. Even then there may be compensations (for instance, the Gellért's wonderful spa makes up for its less pleasing bedrooms). The newly built hotels all meet the highest European standards (the 5-star Grand Hotel Corvinus Kempinski, opened in 1992, and the delightful Thermal Aquincum in Old Buda, for example). The long-established waterfront hotels in Pest also maintain a high level of service; one of them, Duna Intercontinental, has been acquired by Marriott Hotels.

The following price structure indicates what one might expect to pay for a double room with breakfast in different categories of accommodation in Budapest. Inflation is running at around 7–8 per cent, but the luxury hotels adjust their prices more in line with international norms.

★★★★★ 40,000 Ft or above
★★★★ 20,000 to 40,000 Ft
★★★ 12,000 to 20,000 Ft
★★ 10,000 to 12,000 Ft

Cheaper hotels: 8,000 to 10,000 Ft. The cost of a private room may be cheaper still – it should be possible to find a pleasant room at around 6,000 Ft (probably not including breakfast), and even less in a hostel.

Location

The decision where to stay in the city is likely to be determined by convenience and aesthetics in that order. If you stay in the Buda Hills (for example in the Hotel Olympia at Normafa) the air is good, but you have a longish trek into the city. Castle Hill has the best of all worlds – a lovely situation, cleaner air, and rapid access to the centre; unfortunately, your choice here is limited to the relatively expensive Hilton and the small Kulturinnov Hotel. There are some cheaper hotels in the Víziváros below Castle Hill on the Buda side and one botel moored not far from Batthyány tér (Dunapart Hotel, Szilágyi Dezső tér).

On the Pest side there are two hotels with classic waterfront locations (the erstwhile Fórum, now Inter-continental and the Marriott) and one within spitting distance of the river (Hyatt Regency).

Otherwise, your choice is mostly from hotels in the densely built heart of Pest or along the boulevards. In addition, there are several good hotels beyond or around the Tabán/Gellért Hill area (Victoria, Orion, Flamenco, and Gellért).

The distinguished spa hotel, the Gellért

Booking Agencies
(Hotels, Private Rooms, Apartments)

In the season you may well be greeted at the railway termini and outside booking agencies by private individuals with rooms to let. If you prefer a more formal arrangement, there are various agencies that will help you find the sort of accommodation you require. If you want a private room, look for the desk marked *fizetővendég* (paying guest service). In such accommodation, bathroom and kitchen facilities may have to be shared, and a stay of less than four days attracts a supplement of 30 per cent.

IBUSZ

3000 rooms available!
Main office: Ferenciek tere 10. Tel: (06 1) 485 2767; Fax: (06 1) 337 1205; i038@ibusz.hu Open: Mon–Tue 8.15am–4pm, Fri 8.15–3pm. Closed: Sat & Sun. Metro or bus: 7, 15, 78, 173 & citybusz to Ferenciek tere; or tram 2, 2A; bus 5, 8, 15, & citybusz to Március 15 tér.

TRIBUS

Apáczai Csere János utca 1 (behind Hotel Marriott). Tel: (06 1) 318 3925; www.tribus.hu Open: 24 hours. Metro: Ferenciek tere; bus: 7, 15, 78, 173, citybusz to Ferenciek tere, citybusz to Petøfi tér; tram: 2, 2A to Vigadó tér.

TO-MA

Október 6 utca 22. Tel: (06 1) 353 0819, www.tomatour.hu Open: Mon–Fri 9am–noon, 1–8pm, Sat & Sun 9am–5pm. Metro: to Deák Ferenc tér.

VISTA Visitor Centre

Paulay Ede utca 7. Tel: (06 1) 267 8603, www.vista.hu Open: Mon–Fri 9am–8pm, Sat & Sun 10am–6pm. Metro: to Bajcsy-Zsilinszky út.

Hotel Thermal Aquincum

Hotels
Luxury Hotels

The last word in luxury is the **Grand Hotel Corvinus Kempinski** (*tel: (06 1) 429 3777*), in a class of its own for facilities and opulence.

However, the **Hilton** (*tel: (06 1) 488 6600*) has a superb view and good location in the old town of Buda. The three river-front hotels – **Budapest Marriott** (formerly Duna Intercontinental, *tel: (06 1) 266 7000*), **Inter-Continental** (*tel: (06 1) 327 6333*), and **Hyatt Regency** (*tel: (01) 266 1234*) – offer fine views of the Royal Palace and Castle Hill. New, and very central is the **Le Meridien** (*tel: (06 1) 429 5500*).

Mid-range Hotels

Traditional hotels that have been given a face-lift include the **Nemzeti** (*tel: (06 1) 477 2000*) and the **Béke Radisson** (*tel: (06 1) 301 1600*). Two rather soulless products of the 1970s, which nevertheless have plenty of facilities, are **Novotel** (*tel: (06 1) 372 5700*), and **Flamenco** (*tel: (06 1) 372 2000*). The **Erzsébet** (*tel: (01) 328 5700*) is pleasant and centrally located.

wo places with character are the old **storia** (*tel: (06 1) 484 3200*), which has een refurbished but retains its aditional ambience, and the new **orona** (*tel: (06 1) 317 4111*) a Post-Modern building near the Magyar Nemzeti Múzeum (National Museum).

hermal Hotels

. speciality of Budapest is the spa hotel, f which the **Gellért** (*tel: (06 1) 385 200*) is the most distinguished. There re two spa hotels on the lovely Margaret Island: the **Thermal** *tel: (06 1) 452 6200*) and the **Grand Hotel** (*tel: (01) 452 6200*), the latter in a estored building designed by Miklós bl. An attractive addition to the hotel cene is the **Hotel Corinthia Aquincum** n Óbuda (*tel: (061) 436 4100*).

maller Hotels and Pensions

f you want a hotel that is different (but partan), the **Citadella** (*tel: (06 1) 466

5794*) on the summit of Gellért Hill has 11 rooms. The **Panoráma** (*tel: (06 1) 395 6121*) has a nice situation at the end of the Cogwheel Railway. Many pensions are also quite a long way out, but they are almost always homely and pleasant. Economical and centrally located between the Opera House and Oktogon is **Hotel Medosz** (*tel: (06 1) 374 300*).

Youth Hostels

To book a youth hostel contact the **Expressz** office at Keleti pályaudvar (Eastern Railway Station). Hostel rooms are easily availble, particularly in the summer when student dormitories are also available to tourists.

On the Internet information is available at:
www.hotels.hu
www.hotelshungary.com
www.budapesthotels.com
www.budapestonfo.hu
www.travelport.hu
www.budapesthotels.hu

he lobby of the superbly located Hilton Hotel on Castle Hill

On Business

Hungary's transformation from command economy to free market was assisted by the tentative opening to private enterprise under the Communists. Privatisation of profitable or promising concerns happened quickly, but the second stage of restructuring is more painful. Recession has choked off some potential investors, and the unattractiveness of many of the ailing businesses on offer has deterred others.

The Congress Centre

Against this, the increase in competitiveness, even between state sector concerns, is palpable, and many Hungarian businessmen have coped well with the collapse of traditional COMECON markets and the switch to hard currency contracts. As a small land-locked country without significant natural resources, Hungary is heavily dependent on foreign trade – nearly 50 per cent of GDP is exported. Tourism is a major source of hard currency.

Business Accommodation and Travel
American Express
(Deák Ferenc utca 10; *tel: (06 1) 235 4330*) serves the requirements of visiting businessmen. All 5-star hotels have facilities such as conference rooms, fax and secretarial services; most 4-star hotels offer some business facilities.

Estate Agents (commercial property)
CD Hungary
Benczúr utca 42. Tel: (06 1) 351 1808; fax: (06 1) 351 1811.
Healey & Baker
Rákóczi út 42. Tel: (061) 268 1288.

Jones Lang Lasalle
Váci utca 81. Tel: (06 1) 266 4981; fax: (06 1) 266 0142.

Business Hours
The working day is eight hours, usually from 8am to 4pm with a half-hour break for lunch. Industrial workers begin and end the day earlier than office workers.

Congresses/Fairs
Budapest has a large congress centre, the **Budapest Kongresszusi Központ** (Jagelló út 1–3; *tel: (06 1) 372 5700; www.bcc.hu*). Information concerning the various trade fairs held during the year may be obtained from the Director of the Budapest Fairs Centre (HUNGEXPO), X Budapest, Albertirsai út 10 (postal address: H–1441 Budapest Pf 44). *Tel: (01) 266 6000; fax: (06 1) 26 6098; www.hgexpo.hu*

Important fairs include International Tourism (March), Agriculture (April), Information Technology (April), and Medical Equipment (October). A major innovation is the Budapest International

Wine Festival (usually the second week in September), primarily a showcase for Hungarian wines.

Etiquette

Hungarians are meticulous about greetings: if you meet with a delegation you will be expected to introduce yourself and shake hands with each person individually. Business cards are widely used, so take a good supply of your own. Hungarians doing a lot of business with other countries may use the conventional name order, but most will follow the Hungarian order with surname first.

Punctuality is not a Hungarian obsession. If a business partner arrives 15 minutes late, no insult is intended. Business meetings invariably begin with ritual coffee drinking. The decision-making process is slow and the inbred instinct of functionaries to check everything with higher layers of authority is still common.

Money

The exchange rate is fixed daily by the National Bank of Hungary against an average of the US dollar and the Euro. The currency is convertible. Rates are posted at exchange kiosks, in banks, and at American Express (Deák Ferenc utca 10, *tel: (01) 235 4330*). Most banks are open from 8.30am to 3.30pm on weekdays. Exchange kiosks and travel bureaux will change money any time in working hours, and kiosks at weekends.

Services to Businessmen

Accountancy

Hungarian Chamber of Accountants

(Magyar Könyvvizsgálói Kamara)
Roosevelt tér 7–8. Tel: (06 1) 312 4651;
www.mkvk.hu

Office and Secretarial

Irodaház Kft
City centre location. Full range of services.
Révay utca 10. Tel: (06 1) 269 1100;
fax: (06 1) 269 1030.

Regus Kft
The instant office provider, plus video conferencing, etc.
Rákóczi út 42. Tel: (06 1) 267 9111;
fax: (06 1) 267 9100.

Courier

DHL Magyarország Kft
Kocsis utca 3. Tel: (06 1) 382 3222;
fax: (06 1) 204 6666.

Customs Clearance

Shirt Express
Home delivery service.
Kámfor utca. Tel: (06 1) 340 8549;
www.shirtexpress.hu
Open: Mon–Fri 8am–8pm.

Office Supplies

Office Depot
The branch in the Polus Centre shopping Mall is open daily.
Tel: (06 1) 414 2341; www.officedepot.hu

Photocopying

Copy General
Lónyay utca 13. Tel: (06 1) 216 8880.

Translation and Interpreting

FORDUNA Fordító és Tolmács Bt
Multilingual services.
Bartók Béla út 86. Tel: (06 1) 209 2482;
fax: (06 1) 386 8626.

Intercontact Budapest Kft
Specialist in bank, legal, and technical documents.
Bajcsy-Zsilinszky út 27. Tel: (06 1) 269 1153; fax: (06 1) 312 5408.

Practical Guide

Arriving

Visas

Citizens of the USA, Great Britain, and most countries of continental Europe need only a valid passport and no visa to enter Hungary for a stay of up to 90 days.

Citizens of Australia, and most non-European countries require a visa, obtainable at Hungarian consulates (usually within 24 hours). If you are travelling to and fro, get a multiple entry visa for 12 months.

Visas are obtainable at Ferihegy Airport and at main highway border crossings, but not on international trains. Also visit *www.kum.hu* for visa information.

By Air

Ferihegy Airport is 16km southwest of the city. All flights use Terminal 2A (*tel: (06 1)296 7000*) or the adjacent 2B (*tel: (06 1) 296 5052*). Reasonable deals on flights from London to Budapest (eg, APEX fares) can be arranged through British Airways and Malév. From the US, Malév (Hungarian Airlines), flies direct. The best way of getting into the city is with the airport minibus shuttle, which

Airport minibus

will deliver you anywhere in the city for a ticket of up to 1,800 Ft. It can also pick you up from your accommodation in town to take you to the airport (*tel: (06 1) 296 8555*).

Cheaper still is the Répter-Busz (local bus) which will take you to the Kőbánya–Kispest metro station and then you can take the metro into town. Répter-Busz tickets can be bought at the newsagents in the terminal building and also from the bus driver.

Try to avoid taxis from the airport: overcharging and unpleasantness are almost inevitable.

By Rail

Budapest has three international train stations: Nyugati pályaudvar (Western Railway Station), Keleti pályaudvar (Eastern Railway Station) – both in Pest – and Déli pályaudvar (Southern Railway Station), in Buda. A timetable can be found on *www.elvira.hu* There is a direct metro link to the city centre from all three.

The *Thomas Cook European Timetable*, published monthly and providing up-to-date details of most rail and many shipping services throughout Europe, will help you plan a rail journey to, from, and around Hungary. You can buy it in the UK from some stations, any office of Thomas Cook, or by telephoning *(01733) 416477*.

In the USA, contact the Forsyth Travel Library, 226 Westchester 1, 44 South Broadway, White Plains, NY 10601, *tel: (914) 681 7250; 1 800 367 7984 (toll-free); fax: (914) 681 7251.*

Major car-hire companies are represented

By Bus

International bus services arrive at the new Népliget bus terminal (*tel: (06 1) 219 8080*; metro: Népliget; tram: 1, 1A; bus: 103 to Népliget). There are daily buses from Munich and Vienna to Budapest run by the Hungarian firm of Volánbusz (*www.volánbusz.hu*) and the Austrian Blaguss line.

Eurolines (Victoria Coach Station, London, *tel: (020) 7730 0202*) and Attila Tours (36A Kilburn High Road, NW6, *tel: (020) 7372 0470*) run a bus service from London to Budapest in summer.

By Car

Border crossings on arterial roads are open 24 hours, on smaller ones between 7am and midnight.

By Hydrofoil

Hydrofoils run between Vienna and Budapest from April to October.

(Information in Vienna from Handelskai 265. *Tel: (0043) 7292161*).

In Budapest they dock at the MAHART landing stage of the Belgrád rakpart on the Pest side (*tel: (06 1) 484 4010; www. mahartpssnave.hu*). The journey takes five-and a-half hours.

The Budapest Card (Budapest Kártya)

This tourist card offers unlimited travel on local public transport, free admission to 60 museums and several sights, free travel on the Children's Railway, sightseeing tour for half price, reduced price tickets for cultural and folklore programmes, discounts on thermal baths, as well as in some shops, restaurants, etc.

The car is available at all the main metro ticket offices, tourist information offices, in most hotels, and some travel agencies. Price: 3,700 Ft for 48 hours, 4,500 Ft for 72 hours. For more information see *www.budapestinfo.hu/en*

Camping
Magyar Camping és Caravanning Club
has reductions for Féderation
Internationale de Camping et de
Caravanning (FIIC) members
(Mária utca 34, *tel: (06 1) 267 5254;*
open: Mon–Fri 8am–4pm).

Camp Sites
Zugligeti Niche Camping
In the Buda Hills, by the chairlift
(Zugletti út 101, *tel: (06 1) 200 8346;*
bus: 158 from Moszkva tér metro) and
Római Fürdő Camping (Aquincum),
open 1 May to 15 October
(Szentendrei út 189, *tel: (01) 368 6260).*

Children
Children up to six travel free on public
transport. The biggest specialist store is
Brendon at Váci út 168.

Climate
Hungary has a continental climate –
very hot in mid-summer, bitterly cold in
winter. Most of the weather comes from
the west, but occasionally the wind
blows from the Russian steppe in the
northeast, bringing much severer
conditions. (*See chart for details.*)

Conversion Tables
See tables opposite.
Clothes and shoe sizes in Budapest
follow those for the Rest of Europe.

Crime
Beware of pickpockets, especially in the
Váci utca area, and do not leave
valuables in hotel rooms or cars. Car
theft is a big problem. Do not change
money on the black market.

The police emergency number is 107
and the Budapest police headquarters
are at Teve utca 4–6, but go first to the
nearest police station. The 24 hours
Tourinform office at Vörösmarty tér
(Vigadó utca) has a special police service
for tourists. The Inner City (5th
District) Police Department (Kecskemét
utca 6, *tel: (06 1) 317 0711)* also has
English-speaking staff.

Customs Regulations
Personal effects may be brought in duty-
free. Anyone over 16 may bring 200
cigarettes or 50 cigars or 250g of
tobacco; also 1 litre of wine and 1 litre
of spirits; and small presents up to the
value of 29,500 Ft. Pornography and
drugs are forbidden, as are firearms
without prior authorisation.

The convertibility of the Forint means
that money may be taken in and out of
the country, but large amounts of cash

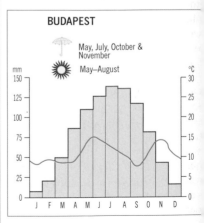

Weather Conversion Chart
25.4mm = 1 inch
°F = 1.8 x °C + 32

over 1,000,000 Ft or the same value in other currencies) will arouse suspicions of money laundering. Antique works of art require an export certificate from the Hungarian National Gallery.

The **Vám és Pénzügyőrség nformációs Szogálata** (Customs nformation Office) is at Hungária körút 112–114 (*tel: (06 1) 470 4119; fax: (06 1) 470 4120*).

Driving

Alcohol

There is absolute prohibition on drinking and driving. Breathalyser tests are common.

Breakdown

The Hungarian Automobile Club (MAK) runs a 'Yellow Angels' (*sárga angyal*) service for motorists in distress, but it can be hard to get through to their emergency number in summer (188, 24 hours). The main office is at Rómer utca 4/A 38A, *tel: (06 1) 345 1800; www.autoclub.hu*). Reciprocal arrangements cover members of most European motoring clubs.

Documents and Insurance

An international driving licence is advisable. Motorists should bring with them the vehicle's registration document and green card insurance. It is obligatory to carry a first-aid kit, a red warning triangle, and replacement light bulbs. The vehicle should display a national identification sticker.

Insurance problems and temporary cover are dealt with by **Allianz Hungária Biztosító** (Bajcsy-Zsilinszky út 52, *tel: (06 1) 421 1421*).

Conversion Table

FROM	TO	MULTIPLY BY
Inches	Centimetres	2.54
Feet	Metres	0.3048
Yards	Metres	0.9144
Miles	Kilometres	1.6090
Acres	Hectares	0.4047
Gallons	Litres	4.5460
Ounces	Grams	28.35
Pounds	Grams	453.6
Pounds	Kilograms	0.4536
Tons	Tonnes	1.0160

To convert back, for example from centimetres to inches, divide by the number in the third column.

Men's Suits

UK	36	38	40	42	44	46	48
Rest of Europe	46	48	50	52	54	56	58
USA	36	38	40	42	44	46	48

Dress Sizes

UK	8	10	12	14	16	18
France	36	38	40	42	44	46
Italy	38	40	42	44	46	48
Rest of Europe	34	36	38	40	42	44
USA	6	8	10	12	14	16

Men's Shirts

UK	14	14.5	15	15.5	16	16.5	17
Rest of Europe	36	37	38	39/40	41	42	43
USA	14	14.5	15	15.5	16	16.5	17

Men's Shoes

UK	7	7.5	8.5	9.5	10.5	11
Rest of Europe	41	42	43	44	45	46
USA	8	8.5	9.5	10.5	11.5	12

Women's Shoes

UK	4.5	5	5.5	6	6.5	7
Rest of Europe	38	38	39	39	40	41
USA	6	6.5	7	7.5	8	8.5

Fuel

Petrol stations (*benzinkút*) sell 98 (extra), 95 (unleaded), 91 (unleaded) octane petrol and diesel.

Shell, BP, and Aral are well represented. Convenient 24-hour petrol stations in Budapest are at Szervita tér 8, Szilágyi Erzsébet fasor 53 (Buda side), and Szentendrei út 373 (Óbuda).

Parking

In Pest you can forget about street parking. There are a few multi-storey or underground car parks in the centre (Aranykéz utca 4, Szervita tér 8). Most larger hotels also have an underground garage.

The capital is sectioned into several parking zones and different parking fees are charged according to the zone – 8am–6pm Monday–Friday and 8am–noon on Saturday. These places are free on Sunday. Parking tickets must be purchased from the nearest coin operated ticket machine for the entire period the car is to be left, and must be displayed behind the windscreen. Minimum parking time is 15 minutes. Traffic police use wheel clamps on illegally parked cars, which may also be towed away. If this happens, contact the nearest police station or call *(06 1) 383 1700/383 1770,* though it is unlikely that the response will be in English

Traffic Regulations

Drive on the right. Yield to traffic from the right unless you are on a priority road (marked with a yellow diamond sign). Seat belts are compulsory front and back (if fitted). Stop for passengers who alight from trams directly into the

Keeping up with the news

road (but you may continue if there is a passenger island at the tram stop).

Trams have the right of way, ditto with buses pulling out from stops. The speed limit in built-up areas is 50kph, roads 90kph, and on motorways, 130kph. A 1993 regulation makes it obligatory to drive with dipped head-lights outside the city in daylight hours.

Notify all accidents to the police and report damage to Hungária Biztosító.

Electricity

220 volts 50 cycles AC. Standard continental adaptors are suitable. 100/120 volt appliances require a voltage transformer.

Embassies

Australia Királyhágó tér 8–9.
Tel: (06 1) 457 9777.
Canada Budakeszi út 32.
Tel: (06 1) 392 3360.
South Africa Gardonyí Géza út 17.
Tel: (06 1) 392 0999.
UK Harmincad utca 6.
Tel: *(061) 266 2888* (10am–6pm).

USA Szabadság tér 12.
Tel: (06 1) 475 4400.
New Zealand (consulate) Teréz Körút
38. *Tel: (06 1) 428 2208.*

Emergencies
General Emergency *112*
Ambulance *104*
24-hour Emergency Medical Service
(English) *tel: (01) 311 1666.*
Chemist (24-hour pharmacies)
Vörösvári út 86 (Óbuda), Frankel Leó út
22 (Buda), Alkotús út 2 (near Déli
Railway Station), Béke tér 11, Teréz
körút 41 (Pest).
Dentist
SOS Dental Clinic
24-hour treatment. Language may be a
problem.
Király utca 14. *Tel: (06 1) 267 9602.*
Doctor
There are 24-hour casualty departments
at Hold utca 19 (*tel: (06 1) 311 6816)*
and Vihar utca 29 (8am–8pm, *tel: (06 1)
388 8501).* Private treatment, including
24-hour emergency service from
International Therapeutic Services Ltd
(Váci út 202, *tel: (06 1) 329 8423.*
Consultation hours Monday to Friday
7.30am–8pm) or Falck SOS Hungary
(Kapy utca 49/B, *tel: (06 1) 200 0100).*
Fire Brigade *105*
Police *107*

Health
No special vaccinations are needed for
Hungary, but keep tetanus and polio
immunisation up to date.

As in every other part of the world,
AIDS is present. Water is safe to drink.
Generally visitors must pay for health
care, whether state or private.

British citizens are entitled to free
emergency treatment under a reciprocal
agreement, but all visitors are advised to
have full health insurance cover.

Many doctors and dentists work
privately as well as in the state sector.
Lists of those speaking your language
may be obtained from your embassy.
The underpaid doctors, surgeons, and
nurses traditionally receive a gratuity
from patients, ranging from 20,000 Ft
for an operation to at least 1,000 Ft for
nurses.

For 24-hour casualty departments see
under **Emergencies**. For non-emergency
dental treatment go to the Stomatológiai
Intézet (Central Dental Institute) of the
Szájsebészeti Klinika (Mária utca 52,
tel: (06 1) 266 0457).

Broken bones are dealt with by the
Országos Traumatológiai Kórház
(Fiumei út 17, *tel: (01) 333 7599).*

Holidays
1 January New Year's Day
15 March Anniversary of 1848
revolution
Easter Monday Variable
1 May Labour Day
Whit Monday May/June
20 August St Stephen's and
Constitution Day
23 October Anniversary of the 1956
revolution
1 November All Saints Day
25 and 26 December Christmas.

Insurance
Travel insurance is advisable. Check that
the policy covers all medical treatment,
loss of documents, repatriation,
baggage, money, and valuables.

Lost Property
BKV Talált Tárgyak Osztálya
(Lost Property Office of the Budapest
Transport System) is at Akácfa utca 18
(*tel: (06 1) 267 5299;* open Mon–Thu
11am–3pm, Fri 11am–2pm).

Otherwise, try the police station
nearest to where you lost the item.
Passport loss should be reported to your
embassy and to the police. Your embassy
should be able to advise you what
further action needs to be taken and
may direct you to the Aliens Bureau at
Izabella utca 61.

Maps
Recommended are the *Budapest Atlasz*
and *Belváros* (Inner City) map by
Cartographia. Buy the current edition
for up-to-date street names.

Media
Local English-language newspapers are
the *Budapest Week* and *The Budapest
Sun* and the new, glossy *Style* magazine.
These and foreign publications can be
bought at city-centre news-stands and
larger hotels. Radio Bridge (102.1 FM)
has some English programmes and
American news.

Money Matters
The Hungarian forint is denominated in
20, 000, 10,000, 5,000, 1,000, 500, and
200 notes. Coin denominations are 1, 2,
5, 10, 20, 50, and 100. The forint is
divided into 100 (worthless) fillér.

Traveller's cheques and Eurocheques
are widely accepted. Banks are usually
open Monday to Friday 8.30am–
3.30pm. There are also currency
exchange machines at some banks in the
centre. OTP (Post Office Savings Bank)
makes no charge on exchange; exchange
kiosks are heavy on charges.

All Hungarian post offices give cash
advance on Maestro, Eurocard/
MasterCard, VISA and VISA Electron.
Look for the *Postamat* sign on a window.

Thomas Cook Traveller's Cheques free
you from the hazards of carrying large
amounts of cash. Some hotels, shops and
restaurants accept them in lieu of cash.

If you need to transfer money
quickly, you can use the MoneyGram[SM]
Money Transfer service. For more details
in the UK, telephone *Freephone 0800
897198.*

Opening Hours
Food shops are open Monday to Friday
7am or 8 am to 6pm; Saturday 8am to
noon or 1pm. Other shops are open
Monday to Friday 10am to 5pm or 6pm,
Saturday 9am to 1pm (but some do not
open on Saturday).

For museums see individual entries;
for office hours see **On Business**, *p178.*

Post Offices
The main post office (*posta*) and *poste
restante* are at Városház utca 18
(*tel: (06 1) 485 9041*), open Monday to
Friday 8am–6pm, Saturday 8am–2pm;
The post offices at Teréz körút 51 and
Baross tér 11C (near Nyugati and Keleti
railway stations) have longer opening
hours. (*www.post.hu*)

Public Transport
Public transport (*see pp20–21*) is cheap
and efficient. It is wise to buy a whole-
day ticket (*Napijegy*), a three-day one
(*Háromnapos jegy*), or a weekly pass

LANGUAGE

PRONUNCIATION
The stress is always on the first syllable.

Vowel sounds
a like the **o** in h**o**t
á like the **u** in h**u**t but twice as long
e as in p**e**n
é as in pl**ay**
i as in s**i**t
í as in m**ea**t
o like the **aw** in p**aw** but shorter
ó the same but longer
ö like the **ur** in f**ur**
ő the same only longer
u as in f**u**ll
ú like the **oo** in s**oo**n
ü as in German f**ü**nf
ű the same but longer

BASIC PHRASES
yes/no	igen/nem
please	kérem (kérek)
you're welcome	szívesen
thank you	köszönöm
(very much)	(szépen)
bon appetit!	egészégére!
hello/goodbye	(informal) szia!
goodbye	viszontlátásra
good morning	jó reggelt
good day	jó napot
good evening	jó estét
good night	jó éjszakat
small/large	kicsi, kis/nagy
quickly/slowly	gyorsan/lassan
cold/hot	hideg/meleg
left/right	balra/jobbra
straight ahead	egyenesen előre
where?	hol?
when?	mikor?
why?	miért?
open	nyitva
closed	zárva
how much?	mennyibe kerül?
expensive/cheap	drága/olcsó

Consonants
b, d, f, h, m, n, v, x, z as in English
c like **ts** in ha**ts**
cs like **ch** in **ch**oose
g as in **g**ull
gy like the **d** in **d**uring
j/ly both like **y**
ny like the **n** in **n**ew
r rolled as in Scottish
s like **sh** in **sh**ip
sz like **s** in **s**ea
t as in si**t**
ty like the **tti** in pre**tti**er
zs like the **s** in plea**s**ure.

NUMBERS
1	egy	**6**	hat
2	kettő	**7**	hét
3	három	**8**	nyolc
4	négy	**9**	kilenc
5	őt	**10**	tiz

DAYS OF THE WEEK
Monday	hétfő
Tuesday	kedd
Wednesday	szerda
Thursday	csűtőrtők
Friday	péntek
Saturday	szombat
Sunday	vasárnap

TIME
today	ma
yesterday	tegnap
tomorrow	holnap
day	nap
week	hét
month	hónap
year	év

(*Hetijegy*), valid on all forms of transport. A monthly pass (*Havijegy*) requires a photograph. Season tickets are available at the larger metro stations. Individual journey tickets must be validated on trams, trolley buses, and at the entrance to the stations of metro lines. Check if your ticket needs to be revalidated when you change trains.

Public transport runs between 4 or 5am and around 11pm, but there are night routes (marked with É on the stops concerned) for some buses. HÉV suburban trains are useful for visiting Szentendre (*see pp130–31*) and Ráckeve (*see pp136–7*). Tickets for Budapest transport are valid on HÉV lines as far as the city boundary.

The *Centre of Budapest* map and the *Transport Network* map are very useful. Timetables are posted at the stops and can also be got from *www.bkv.hu* Sometimes the same numbers apply to two different bus lines. The black number is for the 'slow' line, the red for the 'fast' line with fewer stops and, sometimes, a different route and terminus.

Taxis

The most reliable and economic are: **Főtaxi** *(tel: (06 1) 222 2222)*, **Volántaxi** *(tel: (06 1) 433 3322)*, and **City Taxi** *(tel: (01) 211 1111)*. Avoid freelancers.

Telephones

The area code for Budapest city is 1 (not to be used from within the city); and 06 for calls inside the country; from elsewhere in Hungary to Budapest dial 06 1 before the local 7-digit numbers. For calls between towns in Hungary dial 06, then the town area code, then the local number. Dial 198 for domestic enquiries, and 199 for international enquiries.

For calls abroad, first dial 00. The international operator is 09. Country codes: **Australia** *61*, **Ireland** *353*, **New Zealand** *64*, **UK** *44*, **USA**, and **Canada** *1*.

Phonecards are available from post offices, but many booths take only coins.

The Thomas Cook Rechargeable Prepaid Phonecard is a pre-paid telephone card supported by 24-hour multilingual customer service. Available from Thomas Cook branches in the UK, the card can be recharged by calling the customer service unit and quoting your credit card number.

Time

Hungary is one hour ahead of GMT (Greenwich Mean Time), six hours ahead of EST (Eastern Standard Time), and nine ahead of PST (Pacific Standard Time). Add one hour for summer time (April to September).

Tipping

Porters, maids, cloakroom attendants, guides, garage attendants, waiters, and gypsy violinists will all expect tips of between 100 and 500 Ft (10 to 15 per cent for waiters and taxi drivers).

Toilets

There are plenty of public toilets in Budapest. Cafés, restaurants or hotels tend to be cleaner. Leave a few forints in the saucer by the door. Signs – *mosdó* (WC); *férfi* (men); *női* (women).

Tourist Information

Everything you want to know about travel and events in Budapest and

Hungary can be answered by TOURINFORM (Sütő utca 2, 50m from Deák Ferenc tér metro, open daily from 8am to 8pm). The friendly staff are multilingual. Note that this is not a booking office.

The Tourinform main office, open daily 24 hours, is at Vörösmarty tér (entrance from Vidagó utca 6). Also see *www.hungarytourism.hu* *www.touinform.hu* Tourinform call centre (24 hours) *(06 1) 438 8080*. Tourinform hotline (24 hours) from abroad *+ 36 60 55 0044*; from Hungary (toll free) *06 80 66 0044*.

The Budapest Tourist Board (*tel: 06 1) 266 7477; www.budapestinfo.hu/en* also has information offices at: Liszt ferenc tér 11, *tel: (06 1) 322 4098*; Tárnok utca 9–11, *tel: (06 1) 488 0453*; at the Western Railway Station at platform 10, *tel: (061) 302 8580*; and on the M1 and M7 motorways by the AGIP complex.

Travellers with Disabilities

Facilities for the disabled are generally poor. Information is available from the Hungarian Disabled Association (MEOSZ) (San Marco utca 76, *tel: (06 1) 388 5529*; open: Mon–Fri 8am–4pm).

Budapest Metro

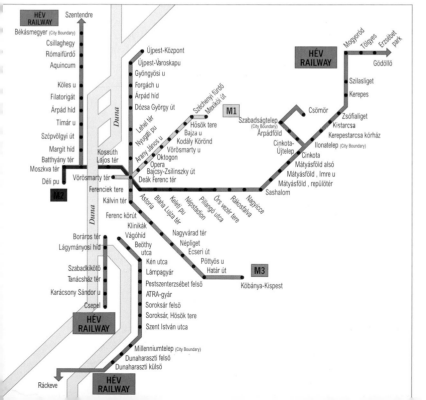

ACKNOWLEDGEMENTS
Thomas Cook Publishing wishes to thank the following photographers, libraries and associations for their assistance in the preparation of this book.

ARDEA 159b
NAGY ATTILA GYÖRGY 18, 171
PICTURES COLOUR LIBRARY spine
TOURISM OFFICE OF BUDAPEST 3, 50, 73, 74, 75, 76, 77, 81, 84, 146

The remaining pictures are held in the AA PHOTO LIBRARY and were taken by: KEN PATTERSON, with the exception of pages 13, 21, 26, 29, 124, which were taken by ERIC MEACHER, and pages 9, 19, 20b, 27, 60b, 89, 129, 137, 166b, 177, 181, taken by PETER WILSON.

FOR LABURNUM TECHNOLOGIES

Design Director	Alpana Khare	**Photo Editor**	Manju Singhal
Series Director	Razia Grover	**DTP Designer**	Harish Aggarwal
Editors	Madhumadhavi Singh, Rajiv Jayaram	**CD Editor**	Arfin Zukof
Designer	Neeraj Aggarwal	**CD Designer**	Sudhir Horo

Updating and additional research on this edition was done by Nagy Attila György.
Thanks to Marie Lorimer for the Index.